LIFE'S LITTLE NUGGETS FROM THE BOOK OF GENESIS

LIFE'S LITTLE NUGGETS FROM THE BOOK OF GENESIS

JESSIE WALKER

Superior Publishing LLC.

CONTENTS

INTRODUCTION		1
1	TRUST ISSUES	3
2	THE PROMISE	9
3	YOU WANT ME TO DO WHAT?	14
4	MAKING DECISIONS	19
5	THE THINGS WE DO	25
6	IN SEARCH OF LOVE	34
7	THE JOURNEY HOME	44
8	REVENGE	50
9	FORGIVENESS	55
10	THE DREAMER	61
11	THE INTERPRETATION	68
12	FULFILLMENT OF THE DREAM	75
13	FULL CIRCLE	88

Copyright © 2022 by Jessie Walker

All rights reserved. No part of this book may be reproduced in any manner whatsoever without written permission except in the case of brief quotations embodied in critical articles and reviews.

SUPERIOR PUBLISHING LLC, 2022
CEDAR BLUFF, MS
(662) 295-9893
Superiorpub@yahoo.com

INTRODUCTION

LIFE'S LITTLE NUGGET FROM THE BOOK OF GENESIS

One day as I was reading the book of Genesis for probably the hundredth time, I started to notice that Genesis isn't just about the beginning of mankind. The very first book of the Bible is filled with all kinds of things we experience every day. There are some things in this book that each of us has experienced at some point in our lives. In several chapters, and I do mean several, I found myself.

Genesis deals with real life experiences such as:
How to deal with disappointment
How do you trust again once trust has been broken,
not only broken,
but how do you build trust in the first place
Issues of sibling rivalry
Unforgiveness and forgiveness
Issues of self-esteem and being good enough
Lies, scheming and betrayal
The decisions we make in life

This is just a few of the things we deal with on a daily basis. Each chapter of Genesis is filled with little nuggets we can use along the way on this journey called life. As you read this book, I hope you will see something in Genesis that you've never seen before and find these little nuggets insightful.

CHAPTER 1

TRUST ISSUES

From the very beginning of creation, God did not intend for us to have to work hard. His intent for us was to provide us with a life of abundance and a life carefree. He provided Adam with a dwelling place and all that he needed was at his disposal. It seems as if Adam had everything he needed except for someone to share his life with. God recognized it.

Genesis 2:21-22
21 So the Lord God caused the man to fall into a deep sleep; and while he was sleeping, he took one of the man ribs and then closed up the place with flesh.
22 Then the Lord God made a woman from the rib he had taken out of the man, and he brought her to the man.

Adam now has a helpmate, a beautiful home for her and all she could possibly want. The first married couple definitely had favor with God. He only asked one thing of Adam. Adam and Eve were now one flesh living the good life. Everything they needed were right there in the Garden of Eden. But one day the blissful life took a turn, maybe the good life was too good for Eve to believe. She, like her husband, had everything at her disposal except for one thing – the tree of the knowledge of good and evil. Knowing you can have everything you want except for one thing becomes a temptation. Sometimes, even with the best of us, temptation will cause us to do what we know we shouldn't do; especially when there's someone in your ear talking to you trying to get you to do what you know you shouldn't.

Life's little nugget #1
Temptation alone with curiosity makes a good recipe for disaster.

God had already told Adam that he could eat freely of every tree in the garden except for one tree. God had proven himself time after time with Adam. He had given Adam dominion over all the birds of the air, all the fish of the sea and over every living thing that moves on the earth. Adam gave names to all cattle, to the birds of the air, and to every beast of the field. He knew firsthand what God had said about not eating from the tree of knowledge of good and evil. Why would you let someone come along and talk you into doing what you know not to do? When we go against what we know to do and what we know is the right thing to do, we open ourselves up to a bad ending.

Eve knew God but she didn't have a relationship with God like Adam. She didn't know Him intimately. She didn't know Him as their provider, their shield from the outside, or the one who keeps all of His promises. When you know someone intimately you trust them and believe they will not steer you wrong. I can imagine Eve having a conversation within herself going something like this,

"Adam is supposed to be the head of this garden, why would he allow someone to tell us what we can and cannot do. If God has given him dominion over this garden, then why would he put restrictions on which tree we may eat from and which tree we may not eat from? All these beautiful trees filled with delicious food is ours except for one. What's so special about this one tree? Why would Adam go along with something like this?"

Maybe, just maybe, that's why it was so easy for the serpent to trick Eve? After all he was the craftiest of all the wild animals.

Genesis 3:1

1 Now the serpent was more crafty than any of the wild animals the Lord God had made. He said to the woman, Did God really say, you must not eat from any tree in the garden?

Life's little nugget #2:

When someone comes along talking and saying what you're already thinking makes it easy for you to go along with what they are saying. Some may even call it confirmation. Trust me, confirmation never goes against God's promises or His word no matter how good it may sound.

Genesis 3:2-5

2 The woman said to the serpent, "We may eat fruit from the trees in the garden

3 but God did say, "You must not eat fruit from the tree that is in the middle of the garden, and you must not touch it, or you will die."

4 "You will not certainly die" the serpent said to the woman.

5 For God knows that when you eat from it your eyes will be opened, and you will be like God, knowing good and evil."

From here the conversation Eve was having within herself probably continued something like this, " I knew it! I knew there was something about that tree! The fruit on this tree is good for more than eating. It really does look good. A little bit of fruit from this tree won't hurt anything, surely. Besides, if this tree contains wisdom, I definitely want some."

Genesis 3:6

6 When the woman saw that the fruit of the tree was good for food and pleasing to the eye, and also desirable for gaining wisdom, she took some and ate it. She also gave some to her husband, who was with her and he ate.

Life's little nugget #3

Everything that looks good to the eye isn't always good for you. For example, an orange may look good on the outside, all big and orange. But as you peel back the layers of the orange and begin to eat it, you may find that it is bitter and dry. It may have looked good on the outside but when you peeled back the layers and uncovered it, you found out that it was not as good as you thought.

Now that both Adam and Eve have gone against what God asked of them, everything has changed.

Genesis 3:17-19

17 Then to Adam He said, "Because you have heeded the voice of your wife and have eaten from the tree of which I commanded you saying, "you shall not eat of it." Cursed is the ground for your sake; in toil you shall eat of it all the days of your life.

18 Both thorns and thistles it shall bring forth for you, and you shall eat the herb of the field.

19 In the sweat of your face you shall eat bread till you return to the ground, for out of it you were taken; for dust you are, and to dust you shall return.

Adam will now have to work for his food because he listened to his wife instead of God. Eve will now give birth in pain and that ole crafty serpent will now crawl on his belly for the rest of his life.

Genesis 3:16

16 To the woman He said: "I will greatly multiply your sorrow and your conception; in pain you shall bring forth children. Your desire shall be for your husband, and he shall rule over you."

Genesis 3:14 -15

14 So the Lord God said to the serpent: "because you have done this, you are cursed more than all cattle, and more than every beast of the field; on your belly you shall go, and you shall eat dust all the days of your life.

15 And I will put enmity between you and the woman, and between your seed and her seed; He shall bruise your head, and you shall bruise His heel."

Life's little nugget #4

Even when we don't understand why God tells us to do something or not do something, we have to trust the process and believe He knows what's best for us and He will never lead us in the wrong direction.

All because of trust issues the happiness Adam and Eve once knew no longer existed. Adam once trusted God without doubt or any reservations. When God told him, he could eat of any tree in the garden except for the tree of knowledge of good and evil, I'm sure he didn't think twice about not eating from that tree. He trusted God.

Like I said earlier, Eve knew God, but she didn't have a relationship with Him. If she truly knew Him intimately; she would have known He had her and Adam's best interest in mind when he told Adam not to eat from the tree of good and evil. He knew once they ate from that tree nothing would be the same again. He knew that once they ate from the tree their eyes would be opened and they would know the different between good and evil. The innocent, blissful, carefree life they once knew was no more.

Genesis 3:22 -23

22 Then the Lord God said, "behold, the man has become like one of Us, to know good and evil. And now, lest he put out his hand and take also of the tree of life, and eat, and live forever."

23 Therefore the Lord God sent him out of the garden of Eden to till the ground from which he was taken.

He wanted to take care of not just Adam but Eve as well. God wanted Adam and Eve to enjoy all the garden provided and to live a life without worries, but because of their disobedience, not only will they not have everything in the garden at their disposal, but they are now banned from the garden. Now Adam must work to provide food and all the other necessities for him and Eve. Adam's decision to follow Eve instead of leading caused disorder, an interruption in God's divine plan for them and it caused them to be displaced. Like so many of us, Eve couldn't trust someone loved her so much that they would do anything to provide and protect her even from herself. Eve had experienced nothing but good things from God, but she couldn't trust that it was real. She couldn't trust that someone was doing all this for her and asking nothing in return, except for one thing, for her to trust HIM.

CHAPTER 2

THE PROMISE

I've always heard that patience is a virtue. A virtue that many of us lack. I've also heard that anything worth having is worth waiting on, but what do you do in the waiting? Waiting is never easy, and it definitely is not for the faint at heart. After years of waiting on a promise from God some may try to make it happen on their own, give up on the promise or just simply say "it wasn't meant to be." Even when we have a intimate relationship with God and know the voice of God, at times it's hard to hold on to our faith and trust that if God said it, He will come through regardless of how long it takes.

Abraham was hundred years old, and his wife Sarah was ninety years old when God promised to make his name great among nations, in fact, he and his wife Sarah didn't even have any children to carry his name on. Most of us probably would have been thinking in our minds how in the world is this going to happen! I'm old and my wife is old, our time of having children has expired.

Life's little nugget #1
There's no expiration date on God's timing

I said earlier that some of us would probably try to make the promise happen on our own, well, that's what our girl Sarah tried to do. Instead of following her husband's lead to wait on God, she decided to come up with a plan of her own just like she thought God didn't already have a plan.

Genesis 16: 2-4

2 So Sarai said to Abram, "see now, the Lord has restrained me from bearing children, please, go in to my maid, perhaps I shall obtain children by her." And Abram heeded the voice of Sarai.

3 Then Sarai, Abram's wife, took Hagar her maid, the Egyptian, and gave her to her husband Abram to be his wife, after Abram had dwelt ten years in the land of Canaan.

4 So he went I to Hagar, and she conceived. And when she saw that she had conceived, her mistress became despised in her eyes.

Life's little nugget #2

Trying to make something happen on your own or trying to fix a problem on your own only creates more problems. Not only did Sarah still not have a child, but she also now has a servant who considers her to be less than. A woman who couldn't even give her husband a child.

Hagar begins to treat Sarah with contempt and she saw her as being of no importance. How great is that for coming up with a plan! All for making things happen myself. Sarah opened the door for another woman to come in and boast about giving her husband something that she thought she couldn't give him. She also created an atmosphere of animosity between the two of them. She begins to speak to Hagar harshly and treats her as if she is the enemy, but the real enemy was her being impatient and trying to make things happen herself. Now that things are all in a mess, Sarah goes to Abraham and wants him to get rid of Hagar and her son.

Genesis 16:5-6

5 Then Sarai said to Abram, "my wrong be upon you! I gave my maid into your embrace, and when she saw that she had conceived, I became despised in her eyes. The Lord judge between you and me."

6 So Abram said to Sarai, "indeed your maid is in your hand, do to her as you please." And when Sarai dealt harshly with her, she fled from her presence.

I'm sure it must have been hard on Sarah waiting year after year and no son. Even when we don't wait on the promise of God and we make a mess of things, God still keeps His promise to us. If God had allowed Sarah's little plan to become the promise, it would have made His Word null and void. His Word is never empty regardless of how long it may take. God kept His promise to Abraham and he and Sarah did indeed have a son, the promise.

Life's little nugget #3

When you've lost hope and have given up on the promise of God, when you can't see the promise being fulfilled, remember, NOTHING is impossible with God.

Genesis 18: 10-12, 14

10 And He said, "I will certainly return to you according to the time of life, and behold, Sarah your wife shall have a son." (Sarah was listening in the tent door which was behind him."

11 Now Abraham and Sarah were old, well advanced in age, and Sarah had passed the age of childbearing.

12 Therefore Sarah laughed within herself, saying, "After I have grown old, shall I have pleasure, my lord being old also?"

14 Is anything too hard for the Lord? At the appointed time I will return to you, according to the time of life, and Sarah shall have a son.

God had promised Abraham that he would be the father of many nations and even through Abraham did not have a child at that time he trusted in the promise of God. In the fullness of time, God kept his promise to Abraham that he shall have a son by his wife Sarah. Just as God had promised, that same time the next year. Sarah was pregnant with a son. The long-awaited promise was now becoming a reality.

Genesis 21: 1-3

1 And the Lord visited Sarah as He had said, and the Lord did for Sarah as He had spoken

2 For Sarah conceived and bore Abraham a son in his old age, at the set time of which God had spoken to him.

3 And Abraham called the name of his son who was born to him- whom Sarah bore to him – Isaac

Abraham allowed his wife Sarah to talk him into doing things her way, such as, using Hagar, her maid to sleep with her husband to create the promise. Then wanting her husband to get rid of Hagar after Hagar become pregnant with a son for Abraham.

Now having to deal with your maid treating you like you're the help and rubbing it in your face that she gave your husband the son you thought you couldn't give him, even though he wasn't the son of the promise. Abraham had experienced what God would do for those who stay the course and stay faithful to the plan. God had been with him and his family from the very moment. He asks him to uproot his family and move to a land he knew nothing about. He provided Abraham with more than he could possibly think to ask for without him even having to ask for it. Abraham and his family lacked for nothing, wherever God sent him he always had favor with God and God caused the people in the land Abraham dwelt to show him favor as well.

Life's little nugget #4

When you have tasted the goodness of God and seen Him keep His promises to you repeatedly, don't allow anyone, and I do mean anyone to cause you to get off track. God is faithful even when we are not, we must learn to wait patiently on the Lord.

Maybe, that's why He rarely gives us a timeline on when He's going to do what He says He will do for us. There are benefits in waiting on the promises of God. When we trust in the Lord with all our heart, with everything in us and we do not lean to our own understanding and submit all our ways to Him; He will make our pathways straight. Waiting on God will test our faith, patience, and trust, but it will also build our character. Waiting on the promises of God is definitely worth the wait.

CHAPTER 3

YOU WANT ME TO DO WHAT?

Imagine waiting for what may seem all your life for something, only to have to let it go. Imagine having to let go of someone you love. Imagine having to choose one child over another child. Well, this is the position Abraham found himself in after years of waiting on a son, he now has two sons. Although Ishmael was not the promise son, he still was Abraham's son. A son his wife Sarah was not pleased with. Sibling rivalry is now in the house and Sarah expects Abraham to take care of the problem.

Genesis 21: 8-10 (NLT)
8 As time went by and Isaac grew and was weaned, Abraham gave a big party to
celebrate the happy occasion.
9 But Sarah saw Ishmael the son of Abraham and her Egyptian servant Hagar making fun of Isaac.

10 So she turned to Abraham and demanded, "get rid of that servant and her son. He is not going to share the family inheritance with my son, Isaac. I won't have it!

Life's little lesson #1
When you take matters into your own hands instead of putting them into God's hands, be prepared for the fallout.

How did Sarah expect Abraham to fulfill her demand, after all, both of them were his sons? I can imagine Abraham was thinking in his mind, you want me to do what? This was your idea in the first place, how can I just send my son away?

When you feel threatened by someone or something, your only objective at that moment is to make it go away. Ishmael wasn't a real threat to Sarah or Isaac, but in her eyes, he was. He and his mother Hagar were a constant reminder to Sarah of her lack of faith in God's promise to her and Abraham. In fact, when she heard God tell Abraham that she would have a son at the same appointed time the next year. She laughed within herself, it was hard for her to believe. Abraham was placed in a difficult situation having to send one of his sons away. Initially, he had a problem with sending his son and his son's mother away, but God assured him that he had nothing to worry about.

Genesis 21:11-13 (NLT)
11 This upset Abraham very much because Ishmael was his son.

12 But God told Abraham, "Do not be upset over the boy and your servant wife. Do just as Sarah says, for Isaac is the son through whom your descendants will be counted.

13 But I will make a nation of the descendants of Hagar's son because he also is your son.

As Abraham gathers Ishmael and his mother's belongings, I can imagine he's pondering in his mind how he's going to tell his son and the mother of his son that they must go. When he approaches the bond servant and tells her that she and her son must go, I can hear her saying, "you want me to do what?" She's probably thinking when I ran away from my mistress because of her harsh treatment toward me God told me to come back and do as my mistress instructs me and now, you're telling me I must go.

Nevertheless, Hagar did as Abraham instructed, she and Ishmael journeyed into the wilderness of Beersheba aimlessly. Hagar and Ishmael were never alone, just when she thought they were about to die, the angel of the Lord came to assume her that God had heard the cries of Ishmael. Although Ishmael was not the promised son, God was always watching over him.

Genesis 21:17-18 (NLT)

17 Then God heard the boy's cries, and the angel of God called to Hagar from the sky, "Hagar, what's wrong? Do not be afraid! God has heard the boy's cries from the place where you laid him.

18 Go to him and comfort him, for I will make a great nation from his descendants.

Life's little lesson #2
When confronted with any difficult situation remember God hears our cry when we call out to Him.

God had tested Abraham's faith and willingness to trust Him in many areas of his life. When he told Abraham to leave from around his family and journey to a place where He will show him, he trusted God. When God asked him to count the stars if he could, that his descendants would be that great even when though he did not yet have any descendants, Abraham trusted God. When God told Abraham to circumcise each male among him in eight days, he obeyed. When God told Abraham that his wife Sarah would give birth to a son in her old age and his name will be Isaac, he trusted Him. After the birth of Isaac, comes the ultimate test of trust, God tells Abraham to take his beloved son Isaac and sacrifice him as a brunt offering. I'm sure this was definitely one of those "you want me to do what?" moments. Although this was a hard thing, Abraham took his beloved son, Isaac to the appointed placed just as God instructed.

Genesis 22: 2-3, 7-8, 10-12 (NLT)

2 Take your son, your only son-yes Isaac, whom you love so much and go to the land of Moriah. Sacrifice him there as a burnt offering on one of the mountains, which I will point out to you.

3 The next morning Abraham got up early. He saddled his donkey and took two of his servants with him, along with his son Isaac. Then he chipped wood to build a fire for a burnt offering and set out for the place where God told him to go.

7 Isaac said, "father?" yes, my son, Abraham replied. We have the wood and the fire, said the boy, "but where is the lamb for the sacrifice?"

8 "God will provide a lamb, my son," Abraham answered. And they both went on together

10 And Abraham took the knife and lifted it up to kill his son as a sacrifice to the Lord.

11 At that moment the angel of the Lord shouted to him from heaven, "Abraham, Abraham!" Yes, he answered. "I'm listening."

12 "Lay down the knife," the angel said. "Do not hurt the boy in any way, for now I know that you truly fear God. You have not withheld even your beloved son from me." Because

Abraham held nothing back from God, not even his long awaited, beloved son Isaac, God counted him as righteous. Not only did God count him as righteous, but He also kept every promise and covenant He made with Abraham.

CHAPTER 4

MAKING DECISIONS

Just when we think we have it all figured out we learn we don't know anything. The nature in us causes us to lean to comfort and familiarity. After all, who doesn't want to live a life that's laid back, stress free, comfortable, and surrounded by family and friends you are familiar with. This thing called life is filled with many twists and turns and decisions that must be made.

Then here comes that thing called life – with its twist and turns. Sometimes easy and comfortable isn't God's plan for us. It's wonderful to be surrounded by family and friends but God always want to elevate us to better things and in order to do that it may call for us to move from the familiar.

Life's little nugget #1
In order to grow we sometimes have to do the hard things, the uncomfortable things, even when we don't understand God's plan. We must trust the process.

Genesis 12:1

12 Now the Lord had said to Abram: "Get out of your country, from your family and from your father's house to a land that I will show you.

Abram was the first man God asked to move from that which he had always known to that which he knew nothing about. Abram only had the promises of God to rely on. Abram was starting in a new place with only his wife who was barren, his nephew Lot, his possessions, and his servants. He had not yet established himself in this new land, but God promised him that he would make him a great nation and bless him. Abram made the decision to trust the promises of God.

Genesis 12:2-3

2 I will make you a great nation; I will bless you and make your name great and you shall be a blessing.

3 I will bless those who bless you and I will curse him who curses you and in you all the families of the earth shall be blessed.

Life's little nugget #2

True trust comes when we operate in that which we cannot yet see. It's one thing to leave all you have ever known yourself, but it's another when you have to uproot your family and all those depending on you. None of the things God promised Abram had manifested yet but none of that stopped him from doing what God asked him to do. That my friends is called "crazy faith!"

Genesis 12:7

7 Then the Lord appeared to Abram and said, "to your descendants I will give this land."And there he built an alter to the Lord, who had appeared to him.

Life's little nugget #3

> When you can't trace God or see with your natural eyes how God is going to fulfill His promises is when you must kick into "crazy faith" gear.

Abram continued to travel south to the land of Egypt, but at that time there was a famine in the land. Abram wife Sarai was very beautiful so when they arrived in Egypt, he told her to lie and say she was his sister for fear of being killed. He was right about one thing; Pharaoh did notice Sarai was very beautiful and wanted to marry her. Abram was about to alter the plans God had for him. Abram's lie got him, and his family kicked out of Egypt. This, what he probably thought was a little lie, had him on the move once again. I believe with all the twist and turns life was throwing at him he temporary lost sight of God's promise to bless him and make him a great nation. God never reneges on His promises. If He said it; He will do it. It probably won't be how we think He's going to do it or when we think He's going to do it.

Life's little nugget #4
Telling a lie will always catch up with you sooner or later. Abram's decision to tell a lie was a bad decision.

Genesis 13:14-17

14 And the Lord said to Abram, after Lot had separated from him. Lift your eyes now and look from the place where you are- northward, southward, eastward, and westward

15 for all the land which you see I give to you and your descendants forever.

16 And I will make your descendants as the dust of the earth; so that if a man could number the dust of the earth, then your descendants also could be numbered.

17 Arise, walk in the land through its length and is width, for I give it to you.

But this promise did not come without some twist and turns and having to make some hard decisions. Lot had been with his uncle since childhood. Wherever Abram went he took Lot with him, but as God continued to bless Abram, things between he and Lot takes a turn. I said earlier that it's wonderful to be surrounded by family and friends, but I failed to mention that sometimes it's also complicated.

Genesis 13:5-7

5 Lot also, who went with Abram, had flocks and herds and tents.

6 Now the land was not able to support them, that they might dwell together, for their possessions were so great that they could dwell together.

7 And there was strife between the herdsmen of Abram's livestock and the herdsmen of Lot's livestock. The Canaanites and the Perizzites then dwelt in the land.

Life's little nugget #5

There will be times when you can't take family where you are going, even when you have the best of intentions. They just might not be ready to go where you are going.

After Abram and Lot parted ways, Lot decides to dwell in the city of Sodom. A city where the people were exceedingly wicked and had no problem sinning against God. Because of his decision Lot now finds himself way over his head. He was dealing with a type of evil he had never seen before. The people of Sodom and Gomorrah had no regard for God or his people. There was nothing they wouldn't do.

When God got wind of all the wickedness that was going on in Sodom, he sends angels to go and check it out. True to the rumors

God had heard, it was worse than what He heard. Sodom was a city filled with sin. Lot tried to save the angels from the sinful men of Sodom, but they were determined to have things their way. Nothing would stop them or so they thought. Good always win over evil, the angels caused the men to become blind. Lot's decision didn't just affect him, it affected everyone in his family.

Genesis 19:4-5

4 Now before they lay down, the men of the city, the men of Sodom, both old and young, all the people from every quarter, surrounded the house.

5 And they called to Lot and said to him, "where are the men who came to you tonight?" Bring them out to us that we may have sex with them.

Life's little nugget #6
Decisions should not be made haphazardly, quickly, or merely thinking only about ourselves. Our decisions always affect more than us.

Now Abram had favor with God and God counted him as righteous. When Abram heard about the plans God had to destroy the wicked cities of Sodom and Gomorrah and everything in the cities. He pleaded with God to save Lot and his family. Things may not be had been the best between Abram and Lot, but they were still family. God granted his request. Lot, his wife and daughters were able to get out of the cities before they were destroyed but like with most things in life, there's a twist. Lot was instructed to fled and not look back, but I guess the temptation to see what was happening was too much for Lot's wife. As she looked back, she turned into a pillar of salt.

Genesis 19:15-17

15 When the morning dawned, the angels urged Lot to hurry, saying, "Arise, take your wife and your two daughters who are here, lest you be consumed in the punishment of the city."

16 And while he lingered, the men took hold of his hand, his wife's hand, and the hands of his two daughters, the Lord being merciful to him, and they brought him out and set him outside the city.

17 So it came to pass, when they had brought them outside, that he said, "Escape for your life! Do not look behind you nor stay anywhere in the plain. Escape to the mountains, lest you be destroyed."

Life is too hard for us to try to navigate it on our own, and we never have to do life on our own. The different between making a good or bad decision is just one conversation away. Our Father is always ready and waiting on us to ask for His help. God always wants the best for us, He will never steer us in the wrong direction. Remember He will never leave us or forsake us.

CHAPTER 5

THE THINGS WE DO

As parents, we always want the best for our children. There's nothing we won't do for them and their happiness. Abraham is now old, and his beloved Sarah has died, as a father he wants to make sure that his son, Isaac is not left alone. He sends his servant to find Isaac a wife from his homeland. God instructed Abraham earlier to not let Isaac marry any of the women of Canaan. Many years have now passed since God promised Abraham to make him the father of many nations.

Genesis 24:3-4, 7
3 and I will make you swear by the Lord, the God of heaven and the God of the earth, that you will not take a wife for my son from the daughters of the Canaanites, among whom I dwell.
4 but you shall go to my country and to my family and take a wife for my son Isaac.
7 The Lord God of heaven, who took me from my father's house and from the land of my family and who spoke to me and swore to me saying, "to your descendants I give this land, He

will send His angel before you and you shall take a wife for my son from there."

One thing Abraham knew about God is that He always keep His promises. He also had learned that when God asks you to do something that's far above your understanding, it's always for your benefit. There's always a reason behind it.

Life's little nugget #1
God is a God of purpose

God basically hand-picked Isaac's wife for him. When Abraham's servant set out to find a wife for Isaac, he asked God to direct him to the right woman. He asked for specific signs from God. God can do the same thing for us when picking a husband or wife if we only allow Him.

Genesis 24: 12, 14-15

12 Then he said, "O Lord God of my master Abraham, please give me success this day, and show kindness to my master Abraham.

14 Now let it be that the young woman to whom I say, "please let down your pitcher that I may drink, and she says, "drink and I will also give your camels a drink – let her be the one You have appointed for your servant Isaac. And by this I will know that You have shown kindness to my master.

Life little nugget #2
God is our guide. He will guide our footsteps if we allow Him.

Not only did God guide Abraham's servant to the right woman, but He had already prepared Rebekah's heart to accept the offer.

It was as if she was listening to the prayers of Abraham's servant. Everything he asked, God delivered, assuring the servant he had the right one. Mission accomplished.

Genesis 24:17-21

17 And the servant ran to meet her and said, "please let me drink a little water from your pitcher."

18 So she said, "drink, my lord." Then she quickly let her pitcher down to her hand and gave him a drink.

19 And when she had finished giving him a drink, she said, "I will draw water for your camels also, until they have finished drinking."

20 Then she quickly emptied her pitcher into the trough, ran back to the well for all his camels.

21 And the man, wondering at her, remained silent so as to know whether the Lord had made his journey prosperous or not.

As Isaac was meditating in the field he looked up and saw the servant in a distance. As Rebekah approached, she also lifted up her eyes and saw Isaac. It was as if there was an instant attraction. That very day Isaac took Rebekah as his wife. Isaac and Rebekah were a perfect mate for each other. God does all thing well.

Genesis 24:67

67 Then Isaac brought her into his mother Sarah's tent and he took Rebekah and she became his wife, and he loved her. So, Isaac was comforted after his mother's death.

All seem to be going well for Isaac and Rebekah except for the fact that they had no children. Isaac prayed to God for his wife to conceive. The Lord heard Isaac's prayer.

Genesis 25:21

21 Now Isaac pleaded with the Lord for his wife, because she was barren, and the Lord granted his plea, and Rebekah his wife conceived.

Life's little nugget #4
Whenever we take our request to God, He hears, and He answers.

As women, we all hope for a smooth pregnancy and delivery, but we don't always get what we want. Everything doesn't always go as plan. As Rebekah's pregnancy progressed, she notices that something wasn't quite right, so she inquired of the Lord for answers.

Genesis 25:23-24

23 And the Lord said to her, "two nations are in your womb, two people shall be separated from your body. One people shall be stronger than the other, and the older shall serve the younger."

24 So when her days were fulfilled for her to give birth, indeed there were twins in her womb.

When God gave Rebekah her answer, she may not have understood at the time exactly what God was talking about, but it soon became clear. From the time Esau and Jacob shared space in their mother's womb, they were always at odds with each other. As parents Isaac and Rebekah didn't help matters by each picking a child as their own personal possession. I'm not sure how as parents you can have a favorite child. How do you love one child over the other child when they're both your children?

Genesis 25:27-28

27 So the boys grew, and Esau was a skillful hunter, a man of the field, but Jacob was a mild man, dwelling in tents.

28 And Isaac loved Esau because he ate of his game, but Rebekah loved Jacob.

I understand one child may be more obedient than the other, one child may be easier to raise than the other, but the love for both should be the same as parents. When God entrust us with the blessing of children it's our job to treasure that blessing. It's our job as parents to assure our children that if they can't find love anywhere else, they can always find it with us. Not only should we as parents make sure our children know they are loved by us, but we should also teach our children the value of family and self-worth. If you place no value on yourself and have no appreciation for what you have, you will easily let go of it without a fight or a second thought. Promoting love among siblings hopefully will keep that ugly monster called sibling rivalry out the camp. Once sibling rivalry enters the camp, it's hard to evict it. Not only was Esau and Jacob brothers, but they were twins.

Genesis 25:29-34

29 Now Jacob cooked a stew and Esau came in from the field and he was weary.

30 And Esau said to Jacob, "please feed me with that same red stew, for I am weary." Therefore, his name was called Edom.

31 But Jacob said, "sell me your birthright as of this day."

32 And Esau said, "look, I am about to die, so what is this birthright to me?"

33 Then Jacob said, "swear to me as of this day." So he swore to him, and sold his birthright to Jacob.

34 and Jacob gave Esau bread and stew of lentils, then he ate and drank, arose, and went his way. Thus Esau despised his birthright.

Esau didn't value his birthright, so it was easy for him to give it over to Jacob for food. Jacob understood the value in being the first born. When he saw an opportunity to grab the gift of the birthright, he took it without hesitation.

Life's little nugget #5
When we place no value on the things of God, you not only dishonor yourself but more importantly, you dishonor God.

As Isaac grew old, he wanted to leave a blessing to his first-born Esau, his favorite son. He was old and could not see at this time, so he depended on voice recognition and Esau's hairy skin to tell the difference between his two sons. He calls Esau to himself one day and tells him to go out and hunt game and prepare him a meal just the way he liked it so he may bless him.

Unbeknown to him, his wife Rebekah was listening as well. She called Jacob and put a plan in motion to trick Isaac in order that her favorite son may get the blessing instead. All for teaching our children honesty, integrity, and loyalty. As I said earlier, some parents will do anything for our children to ensure they have the best. If you must steal the blessing from one child to ensure your favorite child, get the blessing you think he deserve, so be it!

Genesis 27:8-10
8 Now therefore, my son, obey my voice according to what I command you.

9 Go now to the flock and bring me from there two choice kids of the goats, and I will make savory food from them for your father, such as he loves.

10 Then you shall take it to your father, that he may eat it, and that he may bless you before his death.

Rebekah had everything planned out. In my mind I'm thinking she has spent a lot of time thinking about it probably from the time of Esau and Jacob's birth. She was just waiting for the opportune time to put her plan in motion.

Genesis 27:11-13, 15-16

11 And Jacob said to Rebekah his mother, "look, Esau my brother is a hairy man, and I am a smooth-skinned man.

12 Perhaps my father will feel me, and I shall seem to be a deceiver to him, and I shall bring a curse on myself and not a blessing.

13 But his mother said to him, "let your curse be on me, my son, only obey my voice, and go, get them for me.

15 Then Rebekah took the choice clothes of her elder son Esau, which were with her in the house, and put them on Jacob her younger son.

16 And she put the skins of the kids of the goats on his hands and on the smooth part of his neck.

What an elaborate plan Rebekah developed to ensure her chosen son would receive the blessing of his father. Jacob may have appeared to not want to go along with his mother's plan to trick his father, but he soon got over it. In fact, he was pretty good at tricking his father. He played the part and got what he wanted once again. As Jacob approaches, his father Isaac his father begins to question him. Maybe he knew something was up. Something just wasn't sitting right with Isaac. His sight may have been gone but his intuition was kicking in.

Genesis 27:21-27

21 Isaac said to Jacob, "please come near that I may feel you my son, whether you are really my son Esau or not."

22 So Jacob went near to Isaac his father, and he felt him and said, "the voice is Jacob's voice, but the hands are the hands of Esau."

23 And he did not recognize him, because his hands were hairy like his brother Esau's

hands, so he blessed him.

24 Then he said, "are you really my son Esau?" He said, "I am."

25 He said, "bring it near to me, and I will eat of my son's game, so that my soul may

bless you." So he brought it near to him, and he ate, and he brought him wine, and he

drank.

26 Then his father Isaac said to him, "come near now and kiss me, my son."

27 And he came near and kissed him, and he smelled the smell of his clothing, and blessed him and said: "surely, the smell of my son is like the smell of a field which the Lord has blessed.

Behold, Rebekah's plan was a success! Jacob once again received the blessing that rightfully belonged to his brother Esau, only this time instead of tricking his brother, he tricked his father. Isaac and Rebekah were once a united team that worked together, moved together as one, but they allowed the children to divide and conquer.

THE STOLEN BLESSING
Genesis 27:28-29

28 Therefore may God give you of the dew of heaven, of the fatness of the earth, and plenty of grain and wine.

29 Let peoples serve you, and nations bow down to you. Be master over your brethren and let your mother's sons bow down to you. Cursed be everyone who curses you, and blessed be those who bless you.

After hunting and preparing his father's food just the way he likes it Esau takes the food to his father Jacob. As he approaches his father with the food, his father begins to question him and at that moment Esau realizes his brother Jacob has once again received what was rightfully his, he becomes angry and vows to kill his brother.

Once Again, Rebekah gets wind of what's going on and devises a plan to send Jacob to safety until his brother calms down.

Life's little nugget #6
The world is filled with people who will use tricks, lies, and schemes to take advantage of you to get what they want. But if God is with you, it doesn't matter what happens He will always provide for you.

Jacob may not have gotten his blessing the right way, but God was in the plan. He allowed it to happen that way. From the very beginning when Esau and Jacob were still in their mother's womb God said the older will serve the younger. God's ways are not like our ways. There are few times in life we will understand what God is doing at the time He is doing it. Who can understand one parent loving one child over another and plotting and scheming to ensure the child you favor always has an advantage over the other? God strategically designed it that way from the beginning. His thoughts are not like our thoughts and His ways are not like our ways. Like I've said time and time again, we must trust the process and the one with the Master plan.

CHAPTER 6

IN SEARCH OF LOVE

I Corinthians 13:4-6 says Love is patient, love is kind, it does not envy, it does not boast, it is not proud. It does not dishonor others, it is not self-seeking, it is not easily angered, it keeps no record of wrongs. Love does not delight in evil but rejoices with the truth. It always protects, always trusts, always hopes, always preservers.

We all have a human desire to be loved. Some search a lifetime looking for that person. At times we even lose ourselves in the search for love. We expect for our love to be reciprocated, but that's not always the case. Sometimes the one we love, no matter what we do to gain their love, that person just can't return that love.

Jacob has now journeyed to his Uncle Laban's house as instructed by his mother Rebekah. Upon arriving at his uncle's house, he meets Rachel. He has an instant attraction to her. Rachel was very beautiful. Jacob stays with Laban and work for him. After working about a month for Laban he asks Jacob what his wages are for working for him.

Genesis 29:15, 18

15 Laban said to him, "just because you are a relative of mine, should you work for me for nothing? Tell me what your wages should be."

18 Jacob was in love with Rachel and said, "I'll work for you seven years in return for your younger daughter Rachel."

That sounds like a fair deal. How many have heard the saying, "all is fair in love and war?" That saying couldn't be truer with Laban because it really means a situation in which people do not follow the usual rules of behavior and do things that are normally considered unfair. Laban had two daughters, Leah and Rachel. Leah was the older of the two and as custom would have it doing those days, the older daughter was to marry before the younger daughter. Leah had weak eyes and Rachel was beautiful. Jacob's heart was toward Rachel, and he was willing to work seven years for her.

Life little nugget #1

Love should not hurt, if the person you are with talk harshly to you, is very impatient with you, tries to shut your voice down, make you feel as if you must lower your standards to be with them, doesn't make you feel safe and secure, that my friend is not love. Love should not make you feel unwanted and that you are not good enough.

Genesis 29:18-21

18 Jacob was in love with Rachel and said, "I'll work for you seven years in return for your younger daughter Rachel."

19 Laban said, "it's better that I give her to you than to some other man. Stay here with me."

20 So Jacob served seven years to get Rachel, but they seemed like only a few days to him because of his love for her.

21 Then Jacob said to Laban, "give me my wife, my time is completed, and I want to make love to her."

After the seven years ended Jacob goes to his uncle Laban and ask for Rachel. Remember when Jacob was still at home with his parents, and he tricked his brother Esau out of his birthright and his father into giving the blessing that belonged to Esau his bother to him? Well, the tables have turned! The trickster is now being tricked.

Genesis 29:23-28

23 But when evening came he took his daughter Leah and brought her to Jacob, and Jacob made love to her.

24 And Laban gave his servant Zilpah to his daughter as her attendant.

25 When morning came, there was Leah! So Jacob said to Laban, "what is this you have done to me?" I served you for Rachel, didn't I? Why have you deceived me?"

26 And Laban said, "it must not be done so in our country, to give the younger before the firstborn.

27 Finish this daughter's bridal week, then we will give you the younger one also, in return for another seven years of work."

28 And Jacob did so. He finished the week with Leah, and then Laban gave him his daughter Rachel to be his bride.

Life's little nugget #2

The same way you mishandle someone else will eventually find its way back to you, so be careful how you treat others.

Jacob's love for Rachel was so great that he was willing to work another seven years for her. When you find someone who captures your heart as Rachel had captured Jacob's heart, you willingly will wait fourteen years or longer if necessary. Waiting for the woman he loved was no object for Jacob.

Genesis 29:30-31

30 Then Jacob also went in to Rachel, and he also loved Rachel more than Leah. And he served with Laban still another seven years

31 When the Lord saw that Leah was not loved, he enabled her to conceive, but Rachel remained childless.

The first wife Leah now has to compete with the second wife, her sister Rachel, for her husband's love and affection. Once again that ugly monster known as sibling rivalry has entered the camp. Two sisters are now competing for the love of one man. Can you imagine the embarrassment of your father tricking someone into marrying you? The reality of having to deal with the fact that your husband doesn't love you and he's only with you because your father deceived him Those old feeling of "not being enough, not pretty enough, and being second best," are all resurfacing and taking center stage.

Genesis 29:31

31 When the Lord saw that Leah was unloved, He opened her womb, but Rachel was barren.

Like so many women in a loveless marriage, Leah probably thinks that if God blessed her to have a child surely this will turn his husband's heart toward her.

Genesis 29:32-34

32 Leah became pregnant and gave birth to a son. She named him Reuben, for she said, "it is because the Lord has seen my misery. Surely my husband will love me now."

33 She conceived again, and when she gave birth to a son she said" because the Lord heard that I am not loved, he gave me this one too". So, she named him Simeon

34 Again she conceived, and when she gave birth to a son she said, "now at last my husband will become attached to me, because I have borne him three sons." So, she was named Levi (now at last my husband will become attached to me)

Leah has now given her husband Jacob three sons, all in an attempt to be loved. She just wants to be loved by her husband, but her husband's heart is still towards Rachel, the wife without children. In the process of trying to find a way for her husband to love her, she has felt misery, unloved and her husband not being attached to her. The fourth time Leah has a son she directs her attention toward the Lord instead of her husband, so she named him Judah (this time I will praise the Lord).

Genesis 29:35

35 She conceived again, and when she gave birth to a son she said, "this time I will praise the Lord." So, she named him Judah. Then she stopped having children.

Life's little nugget #3

Love isn't something a child can materialize or create between a husband or wife. When you take your eyes off of what's important, you begin to lose focus on what really matters.

Leah's focus was on having children in order for her husband's love. Rachel already had Jacob's love, but her focus was on the fact that she didn't have any children. They both had what the other one wanted. Rachel's focus was totally off, in fact, she became jealous of her sister, a woman who felt unloved and not enough.

Genesis 30:1-4

1 Now when Rachel saw that she bore Jacob no children, Rachel envied her sister, and said to Jacob, "give me children, or else I die!"

2 And Jacob's anger was aroused against Rachel, and he said, "am I in the place of God, who has withheld from you the fruit of the womb?"

3 So, she said, "here is my maid Bilhah; go in to her, and she will bear a child on my knees, that I also may have children by her."

4 Then she gave him Bilhah her maid as wife, and Jacob went in to her.

Rachel wanted children so bad that like her grandmother-n-law Sarah, she takes her servant to her husband Jacob to sleep with. The plan worked, it worked so well that Rachel gave her servant to Jacob twice to sleep with. Both times the servant gave birth to sons.

Genesis 30:5-8

5 And she became pregnant and bore him a son.

6 Then Rachel said, "God has vindicated me, he has listened to my plea and given me a son." Because of this she named him Dan (judged).

7 Rachel's servant Bilhah conceived again and bore Jacob a second son.

8 Then Rachel said, "I have had a great struggle with my sister, and I have won." So, she named him Naphtali (struggled).

It seems as if having children had become more of a game between Leah and Rachel than an act of love between a husband and wife. Now Leah takes her servant to Jacob to sleep with him since it seems as if God has closed her womb. The servant becomes pregnant and bears a son for Jacob, as a matter of fact, she has two sons for Jacob.

Genesis 30:9-13

9 When Leah saw that she had stopped having children, she took her servant Zilpah and gave her to Jacob as a wife.

10 Leah's servant Zilpah bore Jacob a son.

12 Leah's servant Zilpah bore Jacob a second son.

13 Then Leah said, "how happy I am! The women will call me happy." So she named him Asher (happy).

Life's little nugget #4

When you don't know who you are, you will allow the events of your life to identify you. You'll find yourself up one minute and down the next, confident one minute and confused the next, loved one minute and unloved and unwanted the next. Eventually, you'll find yourself all over the place and tired.

Who has Leah become besides a woman desperate to be loved by her husband and willing to do anything for his affection? Her firstborn Reuben even notice her desperation and brings her some mandrakes (love apples) from the field. It seems as if she's willing to try anything to experience the love of her husband Jacob even if it's only for one night. But it also seems as if Rachel isn't content to let Leah have her moment. When Rachel sees Reuben has brought his mom some mandrakes, she has to have some, eventually Leah gives her some in exchange for a night with Jacob. Leah has now been reduced to a woman who has to bargain for a night with her husband.

The night proved to be fruitful to Leah, she conceived and bore Jacob a fifth son. She later bore Jacob a sixth son whom she sees as a marriage gift for her husband Jacob. In her eyes this son will seal the deal for Jacob to want to be with her and finally see her.

Genesis 30:14-15, 17-20

14 During wheat harvest, Reuben went out into the fields and found some mandrake plants, which he brought to his mother Leah, Rachel said to Leah, "please give me some of your son's mandrakes."

15 But she said to her, "wasn't it enough that you took away my husband?" will you take my son's mandrakes too? "Very well!" Rachel said, "he can sleep with you tonight in return for your son's mandrakes."

17 God listened to Leah, and she became pregnant and bore Jacob a fifth son

18 Then Leah said, "God has rewarded me for giving my servant to my husband." so she named him Issachar

19 Leah conceived again and bore Jacob a sixth son

20 Then Leah said, "God has presented me with a precious gift. This time my husband will treat me with honor because I have borne him six sons. So she named him Zebulum.

Life little nugget #5
You can't expect others to see you when you don't see yourself.

After the birth of six sons Leah was so sure Jacob's desire would most definitely be toward her and he would want to stay with her, not out of obligation, but because she had done so much to earn his love but the struggle for Jacob's love continued between the two sisters. Leah had done all she could do to gain the love of her husband. She was constantly reminded that Jacob loved Rachel with all his heart and soul. Leah had to live with this fact day after day. Leah and Rachel were living with their form of disgrace. The Lord later remembered Rachel and allowed her to have a son of her own. She named him Joseph (God has taken away my disgrace). Many years later she bore another son for Jacob, she named him Ben-Oni ((son of my sorrow) but her husband named him Benjamin (son of my right hand). Rachel died giving birth to her second son.

During Rachel's days it was a disgrace for a woman to not have a child and Rachel so desperately wanted to have a son for Jacob, it seemed as if having a son even topped the fact that she already had Jacob's love. Jacob have exhibited several attributes of love such as kindness, patient, and protection to Rachel and it didn't matter to him that she had not borne a child. That my friends is real love.

Genesis 30:22-24

22 Then God remembered Rachel, and God listened to her and opened her womb.

23 And she conceived and bore a son, and said, "God has taken away my reproach.

24 So she called his name Joseph (may he add), and said, "the Lord shall add to me another son.

Rachel tried for years to have her own child for Jacob, and she finally had Joseph. After having Joseph, she pleaded with God for another son. Years passed between the birth of Joseph and his brother. After many years God heard her plead and allowed Rachel to have a second son, but it came with a high cost to her. Rachel died shortly after the birth of her second son, and she named him Ben-Oni (son of my sorrow), but his father named him Benjamin (son of the right hand). Jacob now has two sons from the love of his life, but his beloved Rachel is now gone.

Genesis 35:17-18

17 Now it came to pass, when she was in hard labor that the midwife said to her, "do not fear, you will have this son also."

18 And so it was, as her soul was departing (for she died), that she called his name Ben-Oni (son of my sorrow), but his father called him Benjamin (son of the right hand).

The Bible says, "the man who finds a wife, finds a good thing and obtain favor from the Lord." Jacob found Rachel, the love of his life and he obtained great favor from the Lord along the way. From the very beginning when he looked up and saw Rachel, she had his heart. Laban found Leah for Jacob instead of allowing God to let the right man find her. She was at a disadvantage from the start by no fault of her own. Her father cheated her out of the joy knowing real love and having someone that would love her for who she was inwardly, instead she spend her life looking for the love of a husband whose heart was with another.

CHAPTER 7

THE JOURNEY HOME

After the birth of Joseph, Rachel's first biological son, Jacob goes to Laban and tells him he wants to return to his own homeland. Now you know Laban wasn't about to let Jacob go just like that. Laban saw how everything Jacob put his hands to God blessed Laban's livestock increased greatly under Jacob's supervision. God was faithful to Jacob and all he did. He caused everything Jacob did to increase exceedingly and Laban wasn't about to part with that.

But Laban sons were beginning to talk and say Jacob was taking everything their father owned for himself. How ridiculous! Laban had very little when Jacob arrived, he basically, had nothing. God caused Laban to prosper through Jacob. Instead of Laban correcting his sons, he listened to them.

Genesis 31:1-2
1 Jacob heard that Laban's sons were saying, "Jacob has taken everything our father owned and has gained all this wealth from what belonged to our father."

2 And Jacob noticed that Laban's attitude toward him wasn't what it had been

Life's little nugget #1
When you have experienced the blessing of God on your life, don't be foolish and allow what others say stop your blessings.

It's amazing how we can know someone personally and see with our own eyes the hand of God on them and yet allow others to cause us to start treating them differently, all because of "he say, she say." Laban witness firsthand God demonstrate how He was with Jacob and his family and how He provided for them. Jacob was loyal to Laban and worked diligently for him for years. But the time as now come for him to leave and return to his homeland with his wives, children and all his possessions.

After talking to Laban and experiencing his change in attitude he knows he can't tell him that he's leaving, so he sneaks off. When Laban realizes Jacob is gone, he immediately goes after him.

Genesis 31:22-23
22 On the third day Laban was told that Jacob had fled,

23 taking his relatives with him, he pursued Jacob for seven days and caught up with him in the hill country of Gilead.

Life's little nugget #2
When God is with you, you don't have to be afraid of what man will do. When God is with you there's nothing man can do to hinder you. If they try, they only put themselves in a position to bring harm to themselves.

Genesis 31:24-25, 31
24 Then God came to Laban the Aramean in a dream at night and said to him, "be careful not to say anything to Jacob, either good or bad."

25 Jacob had pitched his tent in the hill country of Gilead when Laban overtook him, and Laban and his relatives camped there too

31 Jacob answered Laban "I was afraid, because I thought you would take your daughters away from me by force

The entire time Jacob worked for Laban he was never fair or honest, but Jacob never complained. Maybe he thought that this was his payback for tricking his brother Esau out of his birthright and for tricking his father Isaac into blessing him instead of the first-born, Esau.

Just like he had to flee from Esau, he now must flee from Laban. Laban pretends he's disturbed because Jacob didn't give him an opportunity to say goodbye to his daughters and grandchildren but he's probably more worried that his little gods are missing.

Genesis 31:28, 30

28 You didn't even let me kiss my grandchildren and my daughters goodbye. You have done a foolish thing

30 Now you have gone off because you longed to return to your father's household. But why did you steal my gods?

Jacob is upset because Laban is accusing him of stealing his gods. Unbeknown to him, Rachel did indeed steal her father's gods. I guess when you love someone as deeply as Jacob loved Rachel, you can't imagine them doing anything wrong. He most definitely had blinders on when it came to Rachel. Jacob had so much faith that no one with him had stolen the gods that he went as far as to say, "if you find the gods may that person be put to die." Wouldn't he be crushed to know he was speaking death to his beloved Rachel!

Perhaps we will never know what made Rachel steal the gods from her father's home. We can only speculate, regardless of her reasoning after thoroughly searching. Jacob, Leah, Rachel and the servants tents he found nothing.

Genesis 31:33-35

33 And Laban went into Jacob's tent, into Leah's and into the two maids' tents, but he did not find them. Then he went out of Leah's tent and entered into Rachel's tent

34 Now Rachel had taken the household idols, put them in the camel's saddle, and sat on them. And Laban searched all about the tent but did not find them

35 And she said to her father, "let it not displease my lord that I cannot rise before you, for the manner of women is with me." And he searched but did not find the household idols

This search made Jacob angrier than working for twenty years under Laban's constant tricky, fourteen years for Rachel and having his wages change ten times. God was always with Jacob no matter what Laban did to him and He always turned the situation around in Jacob's favor.

Genesis 31:42

42 Unless the God of my father, the God of Abraham and the Fear of Isaac, had been with me, surely now you would have sent me away empty-handed. God has seen my affliction and the labor of my hands, and rebuked you last night.

The relationship between Laban and Jacob was a complex relationship. Laban was Jacob's uncle, father-n-law, and his boss all in one. They were similar and different at the same time. They both were deceivers; Jacob deceived his father to give him the blessing instead of Esau. Laban deceived Jacob to marry Leah instead of Rachel. Jacob later deceived Laban and didn't tell him he was taking his wives, children and livestock and head back to his homeland. Their similarity also included the fact that they didn't trust each other, but they needed each other for a period of time. Laban needed the favor that was on Jacob's life to help with his livestock and Jacob needed Laban's "yes" to marry Rachel.

Jacob served the God of his father Isaac and Abraham, The Most High God; while Laban served many little gods. Everything Jacob put his hand to God gave him favor and caused him to prosper. Nothing Laban had put his hand to caused him to prosper, which was evident when Jacob arrived. The accusation of Jacob stealing Laban's gods was the beginning of the end for these two relationships. Of course, Laban tried to have the last word. He reminded Jacob that Leah and Rachel belonged to him, the grandchildren belonged to him. And even the flock belonged to him.

Genesis 31:43-44

43 And Laban answered and said to Jacob, "these daughters are my daughters, and these children are my children, and this flock is my flock; all that you see is mine. But what can I do this day to these my daughters or to their children whom they have borne?"

Life's little nugget #3

People come into our lives for a reason and for a season. We may not always know the reason someone has come into our lives, but when conflict after conflict begin to arrive between you, you need to know when the season is over.

For a period of time Jacob was sent to his uncle Laban's home by his mother for protection from his brother. While staying at his home he became beneficial to Laban and his household. The favor of God was with Jacob and that favor was extended to Laban while

Jacob was with him. Although Laban was not always fair and honest with Jacob, their relationship was good for the most part until Laban allowed his sons to feed him with unfruitful things about Jacob. As I always say, things happen for a reason, this was just the push Jacob needed to return home and make things right with his father and brother.

CHAPTER 8

REVENGE

I know that God says vengeance belongs to Him, sometimes the flesh just won't let you wait for God. I'm not saying that it's right to seek revenge on someone who has wronged you. I'm just saying that sometimes the flesh will take control when you're not walking in the fruit of self-control.

In chapter 34 Dinah, Jacob's only daughter, goes out to visit the women of Hivite and she is violated by the son of the ruler of the land in which they lived. In my mind I'm thinking she felt safe to go from house to house visiting the women. She probably had visited the women on many occasions without any incidents.

But this one particular day Dinah's entire life changed in a matter of minutes. As she so often did, she went out to visit the women of the land and Shechem, the son of Hamor, who was the ruler of the land saw Dinah and he wanted her, so he raped her.

Genesis 34:2-4

2 And when Shechem the son of Hamor the Hivite, prince of the country, saw her, he took her and lay with her, and violated her

3 His soul was strongly attracted to Dinah the daughter of Jacob and he loved the young woman and spoke kindly to the young woman

4 So Shechem spoke to his father Hamor, saying "get me this young woman as a
wife."

In a split second the safety and security Dinah once knew was gone. Her innocent was snatched away from her by someone who said they loved her. What kind of twisted love was this? How was she supposed to overcome this violation? Because of the acts of one man who couldn't control himself, Dinah is now left with all kinds of emotions going on in her head at one time. She's left to deal with the emotions of anger, fear, hate, frustration, shame, emptiness, sadness and depression just to name a few from someone who tells his father that he wants to marry her.

Life's little nugget #1
Emotions after a traumatic experience are REAL, please do not ignore them. If they're too much for you to handle on your own seek professional help. There's no shame in getting help. The enemy wants you to think that you're all alone and there's nothing you can do.

When Dinah's father Jacob hears about what has happened to his daughter he does nothing. He doesn't come to his daughter's rescue, he doesn't confront Shechem about the accusations, he doesn't comfort his only daughter, he just simply acts as if nothing has happened; but when his sons hear about what has happened, they fall into action plotting a plan of revenge. Jacob's sons didn't even think about it, they immediately devised a plan to get revenge on Shechem for what he did to their sister. Why didn't Shechem go to Jacob and ask for Dinah before raping her? When Shechem and his father approached Jacob to ask for Dinah in marriage Jacob's sons immediately begin to put their plan of revenge into action. In fact, they didn't even allow their father Jacob to speak, they did all the talking and it appeared as if Jacob had no problem with it.

Genesis 34:13-15

13. But the sons of Jacob answered Shechem and Hamor his father, and spoke deceitfully, because he had defiled Dinah their sister 14. and they said to them, "we cannot do this thing to give our sister to one who is uncircumcised, for that would be a reproach to us 15. But on this condition, we will consent to you: if you will become as we are, if every male of you is circumcised.

Jacob said nothing, but he allowed his sons to take control of the entire situation. He had more to say about Laban accusing him of stealing than this. Shechem thought he had won Jacob and his sons over, all he had to do was to get circumcised and to get his men circumcised.

Genesis 34:16-19

16 Then we will give our daughters to you, and we will take your daughters to us, and we will dwell with you, and we will become one people. 17 But if you will not heed us and be circumcised, then we will take our daughter and be gone 18 and their words pleased Hamor and Shechem, Hamor's son. 19 So the young man did not delay to do the thing, because he delighted in Jacob's daughter. He was more honorable than all the household of his father

Life's little nugget #2

When your life is all about you and what you want, you set yourself up for failure and to be defeated.

Dinah is only mentioned by name twice in this entire book of Genesis, at her birth and during this traumatic event. Every man involved in Dinah's life has caused this violation to silent her.

During this entire traumatic event not one person has allowed Dinah to use her voice. No one has allowed Dinah to speak. Not once did any of the men in her life ask her how's she doing, what she wanted to do. They treated her as if she was just an object and not their daughter or sister who had been violated. No one seems to be focusing on Dinah's state of mind at all or what she's been through. Hamor and Shechem are more concerned about bringing the two groups together and having a share of all Jacob's and his sons' possessions Jacob's sons are consumed with getting vengeance on Shechem for raping their sister and tarnishing the family image. Jacob's sons were more focus on what everyone would say or think about how this made the family look in the eyes of others.

Genesis 34:23-26

23 Will not their livestock, their property, and every animal of theirs be ours? Only let us consent to them and they will dwell with us.

24 And all who went out of the gate of his city heeded Hamor and Shechem his son, every male was circumcised, all who went out of the gate of the city

25 Now it came to pass on the third day, when they were in pain that two of the sons of Jacob, Simeon and Levi, Dinah's brothers, each took his sword and came boldly upon the city and killed all the males

26 and they killed Hamor and Shechem his son with the edge of the sword, and took Dinah from Shechem's house and went out

Life's little nugget #3
Vengeance only brings self-satisfaction, not justice

No one benefited from Simeon and Levi killing Hamor, Shechem and all the men in the city. Innocent people who had nothing to do with the violation that Dinah experienced lost their lives because of Simeon and Levi's rage and desire for revenge.

This act of revenge didn't heal the hurt nor mend Dinah's brokenness, it didn't give her the answers to the "why me?" question that most of us would have, it didn't give her answers to the "what did I do to deserve this?" question, it didn't bring her any comfort, it didn't even at last give her a voice to express herself and what she was going through, it was all just an act of self-gratification on her brothers' behalf.

CHAPTER 9

FORGIVENESS

Forgiveness is a powerful tool when we choose to use it when we have been wronged, especially by someone we love. Sometimes forgiveness becomes a hard thing to do, and it becomes even harder when we feel we have done nothing to deserve the unfair treatment. I have learned that forgiveness isn't just for the other person, but it's mostly for yourself.

There are so many fearful things that comes along with not forgiving. Unforgiveness will affect your health, mental status, spiritual well-being as well as your emotional well-being.

Life's little nugget #1
By choosing not to forgive, you hurt yourself more than the person that needs to be forgiven.

It's not an easy thing, but we must choose to forgive. When we actually think about it, God has forgiven us more times than we can count. Each time we go to Him and ask for forgiveness, each time He forgives. The flesh will give you countless fleshly reasons not to forgive "you didn't do anything to them, they did something to you, they should be asking you to forgive them." "How many times are you going to keep forgiving for them to keep doing the same thing to you again?" "You're showing signs of weakness asking for forgiveness." "They don't deserve your forgiveness."

Life's little nugget #2
Regardless of how many reasons you can justify to not forgive a wrong that has been done to you, you must choose to forgive because we have been forgiven by God too many times.

Matthew 6:14
14 For if you forgive other people when they sin against you, your heavenly Father will also forgive you.

Colossians 3:13
13 Bear with each other and forgive one another if any of you has a grievance against someone. Forgive as the Lord forgave you.

Luke 23:34
34 And Jesus said. "Father forgive them, for they know not what they do."

Jacob now has had many years to think about the wrong he did to his brother Esau. Many years of perhaps looking over his shoulder day after day wondering if this would be the day his brother would repay him for the wrong he did to him. Although God was with Jacob every step of the way during his stay with Laban and enduring Laban's trickery and mistreatment, his own actions was the reason he was there in the first place.

When Esau realized his brother had tricked him out of his blessing, he wanted to kill him, but he never followed through on his feelings. I've heard it said that time heals all wounds. I don't know about all wounds, but it will heal some wounds. It seems as if time has healed some of the wounds between Esau and Jacob. After twenty years of being with Laban, Jacob has now decided it's time for him to return home to face his brother and seek his forgiveness. In preparation to meet his brother he sends messengers ahead with gifts and a message for his brother Esau.

Genesis 32:4-5

4 He instructed them, "this is what you are to say to my lord Esau: your servant Jacob says, I have been staying with Laban and have remained there till now.

5 I have cattle and donkeys, sheep and goats, male and female servants. Now I am sending this message to my lord, that I may find favor in your eyes."

I'm sure a thousand thoughts must have been going through Jacob's mind wondering what Esau's respond would be; especially, when his messenger returned to tell him his brother was coming to meet him with four hundred men with him. Would this be the long-awaited day of dread that Jacob had been fearing for years?

When God told Jacob to leave Laban and return to his homeland, He told him that He would be with him, but like most of us when faced with fear and the unknown, we tend to forget about the promises of God and try to come up with our own plan.

Genesis 32:7-8

7 In great fear and distress Jacob divided the people who were with him into two groups, and the flocks and herds and camels as well.

8 He thought, "if Esau comes and attacks one group, the group that is left may escape."

Jacob was fearing what Esau was going to do to him without even knowing Esau's intents. God had promised Jacob that He would make him prosper and a great nation just as He had promised his father Isaac.

Life's little nugget #3

No matter how things may look to us, the promises of God are ALWAYS "yes and Amen."

He never goes back on His promise. I guess Jacob thought just in case you're forgotten about our conversation earlier, God let me remind you, Jacob begins to pray to God while he's waiting on Esau to arrive.

Genesis 32:9-12

9 Then Jacob prayed, "O God of my father Abraham, God of my father Isaac, Lord, you who said to me, go back to your country and your relatives, and I will make you prosper."

10 I am unworthy of all the kindness and faithfulness you have shown your servant. I had only my staff when I crossed this Jordan, but now I have become two camps.

11 Save me, I pray, from the hand of my brother Esau, for I am afraid he will come and attack me, and also the mothers with their children.

12 But you said, "I will surely make you prosper and will make your descendants like the sand of the sea, which cannot be counted."

After praying to God, Jacob still puts his plan into action. He divides his family and livestock into three sections. Each section has gifts for his brother Esau along with instructions that the gifts are from him, hoping the gifts will ease any ill feeling Esau may still have towards him.

Genesis 32:20

20 And be sure to say, "your servant Jacob is coming behind us." For he thought, "I will pacify him with these gifts I am sending ahead; later when I see him, perhaps he will receive me."

Later that night Jacob has a divine encounter with God. God blesses Jacob and change his name from Jacob, which mean trickster, to Israel which means wrestles with God.

Genesis 32:28

28 Then the man said, "your name will no longer be Jacob, but Israel, because you have struggled with God and with humans and have overcome.

After a divine encounter with God and a name change, Jacob is still not convinced his brother Esau is coming in peace. Like so many of us, Jacob relies on what his carnal mind instructs him to do instead of relying on what he knows God will do on his behalf He divides his family up in order of least important to him to the most important and he goes ahead of them. I guess we should at least give him credit for going ahead of them.

Genesis 32:2-3

2 He put the female servants and their children in front, Leah and her children next, and Rachel and Joseph in the rear. 3 He himself went on ahead and bowed down to the ground seven times as he approached his brother.

To his surprise, Esau runs and meet him with an embrace and a kiss. He was happy to see his brother Jacob. Time had definitely worked in their favor. Esau had forgiven Jacob and although Jacob rightfully through the birthright is over Esau, he bows down to Esau and calls him lord and himself servant.

Honestly, Esau probably recognizes he's partly to blame for what happened between him and his brother. He cared nothing about his birthright as the first born the reason he so easily sold it to Jacob.

Now that they both have gotten older and matured, they both probably realizes they both need forgiveness from each other.

Life's little nugget #4
A sign of maturity is when you recognize you are wrong, and you ask for forgiveness and when you have been wronged you forgive the one who has wronged you and move on.

In this walk of life as a believer, no matter how many times we have been wronged we must find it in our heart to forgive. It doesn't matter whether the one who has wronged you ask for forgiveness or not. We can't allow unforgiveness to take root like a cancer and grow. We must cut it off from the root and live, even if it means we have to forgive the same person seventy times seven times.

CHAPTER 10

THE DREAMER

After the death of Isaac, Jacob returns to Canaan and lives there with his sons. Although he had seen the effects of one parent having a favorite child, he follows in their footsteps, of all his sons he chooses Joseph: the first son of his beloved Rachel as his favorite. He loved Joseph more than all his sons, in fact, he made a coat of many colors just for Joseph.

Jacob had experienced firsthand the results of his father Isaac loving his brother Esau more than him. He saw how his mother Rebekah had to trick Isaac into giving the blessing to him and the rivalry it brought between him and his brother. He knew the results of sibling rivalry and how it tears the family apart.

Genesis 37:3-4

3 Now Israel loved Joseph more than all his children, because he was the son of his old age. Also, he made him a tunic of many colors

4 But when his brothers saw that their father loved him more than all his brothers, they hated him and could not speak peaceably to him.

Life's Little Nugget #1
A family divided amongst itself will never defect the real enemy, Satan.

How many know that being the favorite isn't always a good thing? The target is always on your back. There will constantly be someone waiting for the opportune time to get you. The target was on Joseph's back at a young age. When Joseph was seventeen, he had a dream that his older brothers would be under his authority. Later he had another dream that his entire family would bow down to him. Foolishly, he told both dreams to his father and brothers. These dreams cause the target on Joseph's back to become a bull's eye.

Genesis 37:5-10

5 Now Joseph had a dream, and he told it to his brothers; and they hated him even the more. 6. So he said to them, "please hear this dream which I have dreamed.

7 There we were binding sheaves in the field. Then behold, my sheaf arose and also stood upright, and indeed your sheaves stood all around and bowed down to my sheaf."

8 And his brothers said to him, "shall you indeed reign over us? Or shall you indeed have dominion over us?" So, they hated him even more for his dreams and for his words

9 Then he dreamed still another dream and told it to his brothers, and said, "look, I have dreamed another dream. And this time, the sun, the moon, and the eleven stars bowed down to me." 10 So he told it to his father and his brothers, and his father rebuked him and said to him, "what is this dream that you have dreamed? Shall your mother and I and your brothers indeed come to bow down to the earth before you?"

Life's little nugget #2
Everything that God tells you or shows you isn't to be shared with everyone. As the young people often say, "sometimes you have to move in silence."

Some time has now passed since Joseph told his brothers and father about his dreams, but the hatred Joseph brothers have for him is still there. When his father sends him to find his brothers the sight of Joseph gave those feeling life. As Joseph approached his brothers they begin to plot to kill "the dreamer." Feeling second best, unloved, and unappreciated by your parents is a hurtful experience and no one should experience those feelings from their parents, but to go as far as to plot to kill your sibling is a whole different kind of thing.

Genesis 37:18-20
18 Now when they saw him afar off, even before he came near them, they conspired against hi to kill him. 19 Then they said to one another, "look, this dreamer is coming!" 20. Come therefore, let us now kill him and cast him into some pit, and we shall say, "some wild beast has devoured him. We shall see what will become of his dream!"

Life's little nugget #3
When you allow jealousy, envy, and hatred to enter into your heart, sometimes it will cause you to do the unthinkable.

For seventeen years Joseph's brothers had to sit with the fact that he was the favorite son and now they must listen to this favorite son tell them that they will someday bow down to him. It was more than they could handle. They couldn't tolerate him any longer, the door was opened, and Satan came in. But God was with Joseph and He didn't allow Joseph's brothers to kill him.

When his oldest brother Reuben heard the other brothers plot to kill Joseph, he convinced them not to kill him. Joseph's other brother Judah talked them into selling him to the Ishmaelites instead of killing him. I guess envy, jealousy, and hatred hadn't entered the hearts of all the brothers. In fact, Reuben really wanted to rescue him and return him back to their father, but he was too late. When he returned and found Joseph was not in the pit, he was dis

Genesis 37:21-22, 26-27, 29

21 But Reuben heard it, and he delivered him out of their hands and said, "let us not kill him." 22 And Reuben said to them, "shed no blood, but cast him into this pit which is in the wilderness, and do not lay a hand on him," - that he might deliver him out of their hands and bring him back to his father. 26 So Judah said to his brothers, "what profit is there if we kill our brother and conceal his blood?" 27 Come, and let us sell him to the Ishmaelites, and let not our hand be upon him, for he is our brother and our flesh." And his brothers listened. 29 Then Ruben returned to the pit, and indeed Joseph was not in the pit, and he tore his clothes.

Reuben and Judah stopped the other brothers from killing Joseph, but they were unable to stop them from following through with the scheme to tell their father Joseph has been killed by wild animals. They knew this news would crush their father. They even had the nerves to try and comfort their father, but he wasn't having any of that.

Genesis 37: 31, 33-35

31 So they took Joseph's tunic, killed a kid of the goats, and dipped the tunic in the blood.

33 And he recognized it and said, "it is my son's tunic. A wild beast has devoured him without doubt Joseph is torn to pieces." 34 Then Jacob tore his clothes, put sackcloth on his waist and mourned for his son many days. 35 And all his sons and all his daughters arose to comfort him, but he refused to be comforted, and he said, "for I shall go down into the grave to my son in mourning." Thus his father wept for him.

Life's little nugget #4
Inflecting hurt and pain on another when you are hurt, only creates more hurt and a vicious cycle.

Joseph has now been sold into slavery to the Ishmaelites and taken to Egypt. Striped of your coat that has been given to you by your father, put into a cistern because your brothers hate you and really want to kill you, but instead sell you into slavery, all because of a dream and the love your father has for you. This would be more than most of us could endure, but Joseph was not alone. God was right there with him protecting him and making sure all went well with him no matter what anyone did.

God caused Joseph to prosper in the land of Egypt and gave him favor with his master Potiphar. Potiphar paid attention to how everything Joseph did the Lord was with him. He was so amaze how God favored Joseph that he put him in charge of everything he had. Potiphar's recognition of the favor that was on Joseph's life cause God to bless all that Potiphar had.

Genesis 39: 5-6

5 So it was, from the time that he had made him overseer of his house and all that he had, that the Lord blessed the Egyptian's house for Joseph's sake, and the blessing of the Lord was on all that he had in the house and in the field. 6 Thus he left all that he had in Joseph's hand, and he did not know what he had except for the bread which he ate.

I imagine Potiphar has many men under his authority who had been by his side for years, but he had never entrusted all he had to them. Can you imagine how they must have felt seeing a slave come in and all of a sudden, the slave has authority over them. Talk about a target on your back. Speaking of targets, did I mention that Joseph was also handsome and well build?

Not only did Potiphar notice Joseph, but his wife notice him as well. As time went by Potiphar's wife began to lust after Joseph and on more than one occasion and tried to get him to sleep with her. Joseph was an honorable man, not only did he honor Potiphar, but he honored God and refused to sin against Him for fleshly pleasures.

Genesis 39: 9-10

9 There is no one greater in this house than I, or has he kept back anything from me but you, because you are his wife. How than can I do this great wickedness, and sin against God?

10 So it was, as she spoke to Joseph day by day, that he did not heed her, to lie with her or to be with her.

Every attempt Potiphar's wife made failed, Joseph had down what no man probably had eve done, turn her down and run away from her; and she was going to make him pay.

Genesis 39: 16-18

16 So she kept his garment with her until his master came home. 17 Then she spoke to him with words like these, saying, "the Hebrew servant whom you brought to us came I to me to mock me; 18 so it happened as I lifted my voice and cried out, that he left his garment with me and fled outside."

The well fabricated lie worked. Potiphar is now furious with Joseph and throws him into prison. It looks as if God has left Joseph, but on the contrary, He's right there with Joseph in prison. Even in prison Joseph fund favor with the warden, in fact, he put Joseph in charge of all in prison. The warden paid no attention to all that was under Joseph's authority just as Potiphar once did.

Genesis 39: 21-23

21 But the Lord was with Joseph and showed him mercy, and He gave him favor in the sight of the keeper of the prison.

22 And the keeper of the prison committed to Joseph's hand all the prisoners who were in the prison; whatever they did there, it was his doing.

23 The keeper of the prison did not look into anything that was under Joseph's authority, because the Lord was with him, and whatever he did the Lord made it prosper.

Life's little nugget #5

When you have favor with God there may be targets on your back and all kinds of weapons formed against you, but rest assure NONE of them will prosper.

CHAPTER 11

THE INTERPRETATION

I have learned that nothing happens by coincident, there's purpose for everything that happens in life. We may not know the reasoning behind why something happened but be assured there's a divine reason behind it. Joseph probably spent many sleepless nights wondering why his own brothers hated him so badly that they would plot to kill him. He probably wondered what he had done so bad that it would cause them to sell him into slavery and convince their father that wild animals had killed him.

Life's little nugget #1

Jealousy is an awful monster that's closely related to Satan, it too will steal, kill, and destroy. But when God is with you as He was with Joseph, not even jealousy, or Satan will defeat you. When it seems as if everyone is against you, don't give up, you may have to go through some battles, but you will come out victorious.

While in prison, Joseph encountered Pharaoh's cup-bearer and baker. They both made Pharaoh angry and was thrown in prison. One night each of the men had a dream which troubled them for they had no one to interpret the dream for them. Joseph noticed the men looked troubled and he asked them why. Each begin to tell Joseph of their dream.

The Cup-bearer's Dream: Genesis 40:9-11

9 Then the chief butler told his dream to Joseph, and said to him, "behold, in my dream a vine was before me, 10 and in the vine were three branches; it was as though it budded, its blossoms shot forth, and its clusters brought forth ripe grapes. 11 Then Pharaoh's cup was in my hand; and I took the grapes and pressed them into Pharaoh's cup, and placed; the cup in Pharaoh's hand.

The Chief Baker's Dream: Genesis 40:16-17

16 When the chief baker saw that the interpretation was good, he said to Joseph, "I also was in my dream, and there were three white baskets on my head.

17 In the uppermost basket were all kinds of baked goods for Pharaoh, and the birds ate them out of the basket on my head."

Joseph's Interpretation of the Dream: Genesis 40:18-9

18 So Joseph answered and said, "this is the interpretation of it: the three baskets are three days 19 within three days; Pharaoh will lift off your head from you and hang you on a tree, and the birds will eat your flesh from you.

God gave Joseph the correct interpretation of each dream. Soon after the dreams Pharaoh throws a party for his birthday and just as Joseph told them previously, Pharaoh restored the cup-bearer to his position and the baker was hung. Joseph's only request to the cup-bearer was that he remembered him once he is stored to his position. Like so many of us, the cup-bearer got what he wanted, and Joseph was the farthest thing from his mind.

Life's little nugget #2

Trouble can be used as a tool to test your integrity and character. When you're in trouble, you will make all kinds of promises in order to get out of trouble. Will you say whatever and do whatever it takes to get out of trouble, or will you walk in integrity and be a "man of your word?"

When you find yourself in the midst of trouble, whether by some fault of your own or not, you must learn to walk in wisdom. Joseph was young when he had the dream about his brothers bowing down to him and he didn't know anything about walking in wisdom, but as the years passed and he finds himself in various situations he soon learns all about walking in wisdom.

Life's little nugget #3

As we mature in our walk with God, we learn that everything God shows us has a set time to be shared. Solomon said it best, "for everything under the sun, there is a time and a season."

Joseph's brothers weren't prepared to hear one day they would be bowing down to this favorite son of their father. Jacob may have rebuked Joseph for what he said, but he had enough sense to realize there may be something to what he was saying. Doing things in the wrong timing and the wrong season is a recipe for disaster. Joseph's own brothers probably didn't know why they hated him and plotted to throw him in the cistern and later sold him into slavery.

But like I said before, nothing happens by coincident, this was all God's planning. Two years later after interpreting the cup bearer and the baker's dreams, Joseph finds himself in front of Pharaoh, king of Egypt. This time Pharaoh himself has a dream and no one is able to interpret the dream for him. The cup bearer finally remembers Joseph and tells Pharaoh that he knows someone who had interpreted his dream, so Pharaoh calls for Joseph. Instead of taking the credit for interpreting the cup bearer and the baker's dreams, Joseph immediately tell Pharaoh that he can't interpret the dream, but God will give him the answers.

Pharaoh's First Dream: Genesis 41:17-21

17 Then Pharaoh said to Joseph, "behold, in my dream I stood on the bank of the river

18 Suddenly seven cows came up out of the river, fine looking and fat; and they fed in the meadow. 19 Then behold, seven other cows came up after them, poor and very ugly and gaunt, such ugliness as I have never seen in all the land of Egypt. 20 And the gaunt and ugly cows ate up the first seven, the fat cows. 21 When they had eaten them up, no one would have known that they had eaten them, for they were just as ugly as at the beginning. So I woke.

Pharaoh's Second Dream: Genesis 41:22-24

22 Also I saw in my dream, and suddenly seven heads came upon one stalk, full and good

23 Then behold, seven heads, withered, thin, and blighted by the east wind, sprang up after them. 24 And the thin heads devoured the seven good heads. So I told this to the magicians, but there was no one who could explain it to me.

Joseph's Interpretation: Genesis 41:26-27, 29-32

26 The seven good cows are seven years, and the seven good heads are seven years; the dreams are one. 27 And the seven thin and ugly cows which came up afterward are seven years, and the seven empty heads blighted by the east wind are seven years of famine. 29 Indeed seven years of great plenty will come throughout all the land of Egypt; 30 but after them seven years of famine will arise, and all the plenty will be forgotten in the land of Egypt; and the famine will deplete the land. 31 So the plenty will not be known in the land because of the famine following, for it will be very severe. 32 And the dream was repeated to Pharaoh twice because the thing is established by God, and God will shortly bring it to pass.

With the interpretation of Pharaoh's dreams God's plan for Joseph is unfolding. Young Joseph is now walking in wisdom and gives Pharaoh wise counsel on what to do concerning what God has planned for Egypt.

Genesis 41:37-41

37 So the advice was good in the eyes of Pharaoh and in the eyes of all his servants

38 And Pharaoh said to his servants, "can we find such a one as this, a man I whom is the Spirit of God?"

39 Then Pharaoh said to Joseph, "inasmuch as God has shown you all this, there is no one as discerning and wise as you.

40 You shall be over my house, and all my people shall be ruled according to your word; only in regard to the throne will I be greater than you."

41 And Pharaoh said to Joseph, "see, I have set you over all the land of Egypt."

The instructions Joseph gave to Pharaoh to gather all the food of the seven good years of abundance and store it up in preparation for the seven bad years sound good to Pharaoh. Wise counsel once again finds Joseph in charge of everything and everyone except Pharaoh.

Genesis 41:47-49

47 Now in the seven plentiful years the ground brought forth abundantly

48 So he gathered up all the food of the seven years which were in the land of Egypt, and laid up the food in the cities; he laid up in every city the food of the fields which surrounded them. 49 Joseph gathered very much grain, as the sand of the sea, until he stopped counting, for it was immeasurable.

Life's little nugget #4
When we are faithful to God, we will see the harvest of our faithfulness.

While Joseph was in Egypt, not one time did God allow the weapons that were formed against Joseph to prosper. When Joseph was sold into slavery God gave him favor with his master Potiphar and oversaw everything in all of Egypt, when Potiphar's wife lied on Joseph and caused him to be thrown into prison, God gave him favor with the warden and was put in charge of all the prisoners and everything containing to the prison. While in prison, God gave Joseph the interpretation of Pharaoh's cup bearer and baker's dreams. After being restored to his position, Pharaoh himself has a dream and the cup bearer remembers Joseph interpreted his dream and her tells Pharaoh. Pharaoh calls for Joseph and God gave him the interpretation of Pharaoh's dream which in turn gave him favor with Pharaoh. Each weapon that was formed caused Joseph to have more authority than previously.

Joseph is now in charge of all of Egypt and the people of Egypt are under his authority. Joseph prepared the people of so much when the famine came that there were still plenty in the land of Egypt. When the famine begins to spread throughout the world, even the people of Egypt begin to feel it. Because of Joseph's wise planning during the years of plenty of storing food in each city of Egypt, the people of Egypt were able to buy grain.

Genesis 41:56-57

56 So with severe famine everywhere in the land, Joseph opened up the storehouses and sold grain to the Egyptians.

57 And people from surrounding lands also came to Egypt to buy grain from Joseph because the famine was severe throughout the world.

Life's little nugget #1

Whether wise counsel comes from someone we consider of great importance or someone we consider of least importance, if it's beneficial, it should not be ignored but heeded. It just might be a life saver.

CHAPTER 12

FULFILLMENT OF THE DREAM

When Joseph had the dream of his brothers and his father bowing down to him, he has no idea what the dream meant, and he definitely did not know how the dream would unfold. As the famine begin to spread throughout the land people from other countries heard there were grain in Egypt and they came from all over hoping to buy grain, even Joseph's brothers. Their father Jacob was still in Canaan and the famine had struck his country, so he sent his sons to buy grain. Life is so full of the unexpected, it will take us to places we never dreamed we would go and in front of people we would never have a clue we would be in front of/ Unbeknown to them, Joseph's brothers now find themselves in front of Joseph. Remember Joseph's dream? Well, Joseph remembered the dream as his brothers bowed down in front of him. Bowing before him just as the dream said they would one day do, they didn't recognize Joseph, but he recognized them. However, Joseph didn't reveal himself to his brothers. I'm sure they definitely weren't ready for that or for what Joseph had in store for them! In order to see his youngest brother Benjamin, Joseph questioned them harshly and accused his brothers of being spies.

Genesis 42:6-9

6 Since Joseph was governor of all Egypt and in charge of the sale of the grain, it was to him that his brothers came. They bowed before him, with their faces to the ground

7 Joseph recognized them instantly, but he pretended to be a stranger. "Where are you from?" he demanded roughly. From the land of Canaan, they replied. "We have come to buy grain."

8 Joseph's brothers didn't recognize him, but Joseph recognized them.

9 And he remembered the dreams he had had many years before. He said to them, "you are spies!"

You have come to see how vulnerable Joseph was seventeen when he came to Egypt, he is now thirty with a family of his own. I'm sure never in his wildest dreams he thought the day would come when he would see his brothers again, especially his youngest brother. Joseph puts them in prison for three days, but on the third day he released all but one to go and get his brother Benjamin and take grain back to their families.

Genesis 42:18-20

18 On the third day Joseph said to them, "I am a God-fearing man. If you do as I say, you will live.

19 We'll see how honorable you really are. Only one of you will remain in the prison. The rest of you may go on home with grain for your families.

20 But bring your youngest brother back to me. In this way, I will know whether or not you are telling me the truth. If you are, I will spare you." To this they agreed

Life's little nugget #1
Sometimes we tend to forget that the same measure that we measure to someone else will someday be measured right back to us.

There's no surprise the brothers now remember the harsh treatment they dished out to their brother Joseph before selling him into slavery. The entire ordeal is probably flashing before their eyes as they remember seeing and ignoring the fear in Joseph's eyes and hearing him begging them not to kill him. Now they must face the music for their deeds.

Genesis 42:21-22

21 Speaking among themselves, they said, "this has all happened because of what we did to Joseph long ago. We saw his terror and anguish and heard his pleadings, but we wouldn't listen. That's why this trouble has come upon us."

22 Didn't I tell you not to do it?" Reuben asked. "But you wouldn't listen. And now we are going to die because we murdered him,"

Life's little nugget #2
The deeds we do in life whether good or bad, always, somehow, has a way of coming back to us.

It would have been so easy for Joseph to punish his brothers and repay them for their evil treatment towards him, but instead he helps his brothers. Not only does he provide them with the much-needed grain for food, but he also secretly put their money back in their sacks. Joseph's heart was filled wit compassion instead of hatred and revenge.

Genesis 42:25-26

25 Joseph then ordered his servants to fill the men's sacks with grain, but he also gave secret instructions to return each brother's payment at the top of his sack. He also gave them provisions for their journey.

26 So they loaded up their donkeys with the grain and started for home.

When the brothers realize their money was still in their sack their hearts sink with fear that God is repaying them for the wrong, they inflicted on Joseph. When they finally returned home, they tell their father of all that had happened. I can't even imagine the emotions Jacob must have felt when they tell him they had to leave Simeon and the only way to get him back is to take Benjamin to Egypt. I'm sure as they are telling him the story, the events of what happened to Joseph and how he was killed by wild animals is the only thing playing in Jacob's mind. There's now no way he's about to let his only son left by Rachel leave him, "NOT TODAY!"

Genesis 42:35-38

35 As they emptied out the sacks, there at the top of each one was the bag of money paid for the grain. Terror gripped them, as it did their father.

36 Jacob exclaimed, "you have deprived me of my children!" Joseph has disappeared, Simeon is gone and now you want me to take Benjamin, too. Everything is going against me!"

37 then Reuben said to his father, "you may kill my two sons if I don't bring Benjamin back to you, I'll be responsible for him."

38 But Jacob replied, "my son will not go down with you, for his brother Joseph is dead, and he alone is left of his mother's

children. If anything should happen to him, you would bring my gray head down to the grave in deep sorrow."

Life's little nugget #3
With some, time doesn't heal all or even some wounds.

The wound Jacob has from Joseph not being with him is just as flesh 20 years later as it was the day it happened. Some things only God can heal or make better. Some time has passed since the brothers first trip to Egypt and Simeon is still in Egypt. The famine is still real in Canaan and Jacob and his sons have no more grain left for food. He tells them to go back to Egypt to buy more grain that they may live. Judah immediately reminds his father that they can not return to Egypt without Benjamin. Bringing the subject of Benjamin going to Egypt causes Jacob to become upset all over again. It's almost as if Jacob blames his sons for saying that they had a younger brother at home with his father.

Genesis 43:6-7

6 Why did you ever tell him you had another brother? Jacob moaned. "Why did you have to treat me with such cruelty?"

7 But the man specifically asked us about our family, they replied. "He wanted to know whether our father was still living, and he asked us if we had another brother, so we told him. "How could we have known he would say, "bring me your brother?"

After much back and forth with his father, Judah finally makes it clear to his father that if he doesn't allow Benjamin to go to Egypt, they cannot return to buy grain and they all will die. It seems as if Judah is now becoming a little frustrated with his father's reluctance to let Benjamin go to Egypt in order that they all may live.

Genesis 43:8-10

8 Then Judah said to Israel his father, "send the lad with me, and we will arise and go, that we may live and not die, both me and you and also our little ones.

9 I myself will be surety for him, from my hand you shall require him. If I do not bring him back to you and set him before you, then let me bear the blame forever.

10 For if we had not lingered, surely by now we would have returned this second time.

After much conversation, Jacob finally agrees to let Benjamin go to Egypt with Judah. He sends gifts along with Judah including double silver to cover the silver they brought back with them. That must have been a long journey back to Egypt wondering what would happen to them once they returned. Would they accuse Judah of stealing the silver? Would both Judah and Benjamin be put in prison with Simeon? Judah now has the burden of protecting his brother Benjamin and returning him back home safety. Fearing the unknown must have been nerve wrecking for Judah. Upon returning to Egypt, they are met by Joseph. I can imagine Joseph must have been overcome with emotions when he sees Benjamin, but he somehow holds it together. He tells his servant to take them to his house and prepare a meal for them, but Judah and Benjamin don't know all that 's in store for them. They are terrified, thinking they are going to be killed because of the silver that was put back in their sacks.

Genesis 43:17-18

17 Then the man did as Joseph ordered, and the man brought the men into Joseph's house

18 Now the men were afraid because they were brought into Joseph's house, and they said, "it is because of the money, which

was returned in our sacks the first time, that we are brought in, so that he may make a case against us and seize us, to take us as slaves with our donkeys."

Life's little nugget #4
Fear of waking in the unknown will cause worry, stress, anguish, anxiety, and a loss of freedom. You are now a prisoner of fear. You're afraid of everything. It is now that we must walk in faith that God will deliver us and not allow the enemy to cause us to live in fear.

Fearing for his life and the life of his brother, Judah begins to explain the circumstances of the silver. To Judah's pleasant surprise, Joseph's steward tells them not to be afraid and he then brings Simeon out to join them. The brothers are now reunited! When Joseph arrives home his brothers bowed down before him. Sounds familiar? Joseph begins to ask them about his father and his well being. They tell him that their father is alive and well. Once again, they bow down, prostrating themselves before Joseph.

Genesis 43:26-28

26 And when Joseph came home, they brought him the present which was in their hand into the house, and bowed down before him to the earth.

27 Then he asked them about their well-being, and said, is your father well, the man of whom you spoke? Is he still alive?"

28 And they answered, "your servant our father is in good health, he is still alive. "And they bowed their heads down and prostrated themselves.

When Joseph sees his youngest brother Benjamin he's overcome with joy. He's so overcome that he hurries out the room before he weeps in front of his brothers. After collecting himself, he returns.

Genesis 43:30-31

30 Now his heart yearned for his brother; so Joseph made haste and sought somewhere to weep. And he went into his chamber and wept there.

31 Then he washed his face and came out, and he restrained himself, and said, "serve the bread".

Everything the brothers feared would happen to them, happened just the opposite. They enjoyed a feast from Joseph's table and enjoyed each other. The time has now come for the brothers to return home, but Joseph had one more surprise in store for them. How could he simply let his brothers leave and return home without the guarantee of seeing his father again? Joseph strategized a plan he knew would cause them to have to come back.

Genesis 44: 1-2

1 Joseph commanded the steward of his house, saying, "fill the men's sacks with food, as much as they can carry, and put each man's money in the mouth of his sack.

2 Also put my cup, the silver cup, in the mouth of the sack of the youngest, and his grain money.: So, he did according to the word that Joseph had spoken.

Shortly after the brothers left to return home, Joseph sent his men after them saying they had stolen his silver cup. Unbeknown to the brothers, Joseph had slipped the silver cup into Benjamin's sack. Joseph's brothers may have been harsh to him and treated him badly in the past, but he knew they were by all counts honorable men and would never steal from someone who had been so kind to them. But his brothers were about to leave, and he had to devise a plan in order to see his aging father.

Genesis 44:4-5

4 When they had gone out of the city, and were not yet far off, Joseph said to his steward, "get up, follow the men, and when you overtake them, say to them, "why have you repaid evil for good?'

5 So he overtook them, and he spoke to them these same words.

I can only imagine what Joseph's brothers were thinking when the steward tells them they have stolen the silver cup, especially Judah. He probably can't believe this is happened to them, they have gotten their brother Simeon back and they still have Benjamin, how could this be happening? I'm sure they thought everything was cool between them and the man they had just enjoyed a feast with, especially since they had brought the money back as well. The brothers were so sure that none of them had the silver cup that they were willing to put their lives on the line. Bad idea, the silver cup was indeed found in Benjamin's sack just as Joseph planned. What would the brothers do now?

Genesis 44:7-9, 11-12

7 And they said to him, "why does my lord say these words?" Far be it from us that your servants should do such a thing.

8 Look, we brought back to you from the land of Canaan the money which we found in the mouth of our sacks. How then could we steal silver or gold from your lord's house?

9 With whomever of your servants it is found, let him die, and we also will be my lord's slaves.

11 Then each man speedily let down his sack to the ground, and each opened his sack.

12 So he searched. He began wit the oldest and left off wit the youngest, and the cup was found in Benjamin's sack.

What in the world in going on! Judah promised his father he would return Benjamin home safety and there is no way he can possibly go home without him. Returning home without Jacob's beloved Benjamin would kill him and Joseph is well aware of that. Once again, the brothers bow down to the ground in front of Joseph and place themselves at his mercy. What can they possibly say to Joseph that will cause him to let Benjamin go?

Genesis 44:16-17

16 Then Judah said, 'what shall we say to my lord?" what shall we speak?" or how shall we clear ourselves?" God has found out the iniquity of your servants; here we are, my lord's slaves, both we and he also with whom the cup was found."

17 But he said, "Far be it from me that I should do so, the man in whose hand the cup was found, he shall be my slave. And as for you, go up in peace to your father

Life's little nugget #5

When you find yourself wit your back up against the wall and need mercy, remember God is merciful and show mercy to those who call upon Him.

Like I said earlier, Judah knows there is no way he can go home without his brother Benjamin and Joseph knows it too. Judah and his brothers have tried everything, including offering to stay and serving as Joseph's slave instead of Benjamin. Of course, Joseph wasn't going for that! His desire is to see his aging father and he knows if he let Benjamin go his father will have no reason to come to Egypt.

Judah now has no choice but to remind Joseph how it came to be that Benjamin ended up in Egypt in the first place and tell him that Benjamin is the youngest son of his old aging father. Hoping he will have compassion and allow Benjamin to go home.

Genesis 44:19-22

19 My lord asked his servants, saying, "have you a father or a brother?"

20 And we said to my lord, "we have a father, an old man, and a child of his old age, who is young, his brother is dead, and he alone is left of his mother's children, and his father loves him."

21 Then you said to your servants, "bring him down to me, that I may set my eyes on him."

22 And we said to my lord, "the lad cannot leave his father, for if he should leave his father, his father would die."

Judah reminds Joseph that they were twelve sons of one man, one is no longer with them, one is being held captive and the youngest is the only child left of his mother. Judah goes on to tell Joseph that Benjamin is his old father's entire life and if he returns without Benjamin his father will surely die! Joseph's objective in keeping Benjamin was to see his father, but how could he now go through with his plan knowing it might very well kill his father?"

Genesis 44:27-29

27 Then your servants my father said to us, you know that my wife bore me two sons;

28 and the one went out from me, and I said, "surely he is torn to pieces, and I have not seen him since.

29 But if you take this one also from me, and calamity befalls him, you shall bring down my gray hair wit sorrow to the grave."

This is way too much for Joseph to handle. He can no longer keep the secret that his is their brother. He is overcome by emotions and finally reveal his identity to his brothers. You know his brothers are in total shock once Joseph revealed his identity.. Imagine the dreamer, the favorite son, the brother they hated so much that they wanted to kill him but instead sold him into slavery and later ended up in Egypt, the one who is second in command in Egypt, the one who determines whether or not to sell them grain for food, the one who basically has their destiny in his hands is one in the same. They are all shock and afraid. His brothers are so afraid he's going to get revenge on them, but Joseph assures them that he's not angry with them and he tells them not to be angry with themselves. Since being in Egypt and all that have unfolded while he has been in Egypt, Joseph realizes him being sold into slavery and being in Egypt was all a master plan designed by God.

Genesis 45:3-5

3 Then Joseph said to his brothers, "I am Joseph; does my father still live?" But his brothers could not answer him for they were dismayed in his presence.

4 Then Joseph said to his brothers, "please come near to me, so they came near. Then he said, "I am Joseph your brother. Whom you sold into Egypt.

5 But now, do not therefore be grieved or angry with yourselves because you sold me here; for God sent me before you to preserve life.

Life's little nugget #6

Everything the enemy means for your bad, God will always turn it around for your good when you stay humble, not try to get revenge, and not complain about what's happening to you.

If Joseph had not been in Egypt, he would have never been placed in a position to meet Pharaoh. Pharaoh searched all over Egypt for someone who could interpret his dream but found no one. God strategically sent Joseph to Egypt at that appointed time to save the lives of many, even his own family.

CHAPTER 13

FULL CIRCLE

If the events in Joseph's life had not unfolded exactly the way they unfolded, the famine that went throughout the country would have overtaken them all. God sent Joseph ahead to prepare a way that they all might live. After exposing himself to his brothers, Joseph sent them to get his father and bring him back to Egypt, so he can provide for him and all his brothers and their families during the remainder of the famine. After instructing his brothers what to say to his father Jacob, he has a long-awaited moment with his youngest brother Benjamin and the rest of his brothers. After embracing each other and rejoicing, Joseph and his brothers talk.

Life's little nugget #1
All families have issues of some sort, but when we allow the issues to grow and not deal with them, when we leave things unresolved and unsaid, we only create more issues in the long scheme of things. Things left unsaid fuel the imagination.

When Pharaoh hears that Joseph brothers are in Egypt he is delighted. He not only welcomes them, but he tells Joseph to send for his father and all the family. He gives them the best of everything Egypt has to offer. He even sends the best of Egypt with them on their journey to get their father.

Genesis 45:22-23

22 He gave to all of them, to each man, changes of garments; but to Benjamin he gave three hundred pieces of silver and five changes of garments.

23 And he sent to his father these things; ten donkeys loaded with the good things of Egypt, and ten female donkeys loaded with grain, bread, and food for his father for the journey.

When Joseph's brothers arrive home with Benjamin, they tell their father Jacob that Joseph is still alive and of all that has happened. At first Jacob did not believe them. How could he after thinking for years Joseph was dead, but after seeing all Pharaoh and Joseph had sent with them, he became a believer! His heart was overjoyed knowing his beloved son was alive, the son of the love of his life, Rachel.

Genesis 45:26-28

26 And they told him saying, "Joseph is still alive, and he is governor over all the land of Egypt." And Jacob's heart stood still because he did not believe them.

27 But when they told him all the words which Joseph had said to them, and when he saw the carts which Joseph had sent to carry him, the spirit of Jacob their father revived.

28 Then Israel said, "it is enough. Joseph my son is still alive. I will go and see him before I die."

Previously, Jacob was so filled with fear that something might happen to Benjamin if he sent him to Egypt and that he would never see him again. He was afraid of losing his only son left by Rachel, but within a matter of minutes after his other sons returned with Benjamin and the news that Joseph is alive, all that fear was washed away. His heart is now overcome with joy knowing that Joseph is yet alive! I'm sure he could barely contain himself. He probably wanted to leave that very night knowing the son who he once thought was dead is alive. On their way to Egypt Jacob stops at Beersheba to offer sacrifices to God. While there, God spoke to Jacob in a vision at night and told him not to be afraid to go to Egypt because he would be with him and make him a great nation in the land of Egypt. Not only would He make him a great nation in Egypt, but He would bring him back home before he died and Joseph himself will close his eyes. I'm sure Jacob was at peace the entire journey to Egypt and while he was in Egypt knowing this.

Genesis 46: 3-4

3 So He said, "I am God, the God of your father, do not fear to go down to Egypt, for I will make of you a great nation there.

4 I will go down with you to Egypt, and I will also surely bring you up again, and Joseph will put his hand on your eyes.

Life's little nugget #2

There will be times in our walk with God when we can't see God in the midst of what's going on in our lives, we can't feel His presence, we can't hear His voice clearly, we can't taste His goodness, but know that He's always behind the scenes working things out for our good.

Pharaoh was very kind and generous to Joseph's father, brothers, and all that belonged to them while they were in Egypt. He gave them the best of everything just s he promised. The famine was still very severe in both Egypt and Canaan, but Joseph was a smart businessman. Though his wisdom and know-how of negotiating all survived the famine.

Seventeen years have now passed since Jacob arrived in Egypt and the time has now drawn near for him to die. Joseph takes his father back home just as he promised, and he brings his sons, Manasseh and Ephraim, to see his father. While they were there their grandfather Jacob reached out his hand and blessed them. It was a custom for the right hand to be placed on the head of the firstborn and the left hand on the head of the younger, but Jacob crosses his arms and placed his right hand on the younger and his left hand on the head of the firstborn.

Genesis 48:15-16

15 Then he blessed Joseph and said, "may the God before whom my fathers Abraham and Isaac walked faithfully, the God who has been my shepherd all my life to this day

16 the Angel who has delivered me from all harm – may he bless these boys. May they be called by my name and the names of my fathers Abraham and Isaac, and may they increase greatly on the earth."

Instantly, when Joseph saw his father's right hand on the head of the younger, Ephraim's head he tried to correct him, but Jacob assured him he knew what he was doing. His father before him, Isaac, was the younger but God had already predestined him to be greater than his brother Ismael. While Jacob and his brother Esau were still in their mother's womb, God predestined him to be greater than his brother. Joseph's dream was that he would be greater than his brothers and now Joseph's father is declaring the same over the younger brother. They both shall be great, but the younger will be greater than the older.

Genesis 48:19-20

19 But his father refused and said, "I know my son, I know. He too will become a people, and he too will become great. Nevertheless, his younger brother will be greater than he, and his descendants will become a group of nations."

20 He blessed them that day and said, "in your name will Israel pronounce this blessing; May God make you like Ephraim and Manasseh."

After blessing Joseph's two sons, Jacob tells Joseph that's he's about to die but God will be with him and allow him to go back to the land of his fathers. He also gives Joseph one more ridge of land more than his brothers.

Life's little nugget #3
Isaiah 55:8-9

For my thoughts are not your thoughts, neither are your ways my ways, declares the Lord. As the heavens are higher than the earth, so are my ways higher than your ways, and my thoughts than your thoughts. Our thoughts and our ways will never compare to God's thoughts and ways for our life.

Jacob can now die in peace, the beloved son whom he thought he would never see again is alive. Not only is Joseph alive but he saved the lives of his father, brothers, and all their household during the famine. God allowed Jacob to enjoy Joseph for seventeen additional years that he thought he would never have. God even favored Jacob to see Joseph's two sons and to bestow blessings upon them. What more could he ask for? He's life has now come full circle. But before dying he calls his twelve sons together to tell them the future that awaits them.

JACOB'S LAST WORDS

1 And Jacob called his sons and said, "Gather together, that I may tell you what shall befall you in the last days:

2 "Gather together and hear, you sons of Jacob, and listen to Israel your father.

3 "Reuben, you are my firstborn, my might, and the beginning of my strength, the excellency of dignity and the excellency of power.

4 Unstable as water, you shall not excel, because you went up to your father's bed; then you defiled *it*— He went up to my couch.

5 "Simeon and Levi *are* brothers. Instruments of cruelty *are in* their dwelling place.

6 Let not my soul enter their council. Let not my honor be united to their assembly. For in their anger they slew a man, and in their self-will, they hamstrung an ox.

7 Cursed *be* their anger, for *it is* fierce. and their wrath, for it is cruel! I will divide them in Jacob and scatter them in Israel.

8 Judah, you *are he* whom your brothers shall praise. Your hand *shall be* on the neck of your enemies. your father's children shall bow down before you.

9 Judah *is* a lion's whelp; from the prey, my son, you have gone up. He bows down, he lies down as a lion; And as a lion, who shall rouse him?

10 The scepter shall not depart from Judah, Nor a lawgiver from between his feet, until Shiloh comes; and to Him *shall be* the obedience of the people.

11 Binding his donkey to the vine, and his donkey's colt to the choice vine, he washed his garments in wine, and his clothes in the blood of grapes.

12 His eyes *are* darker than wine, and his teeth whiter than milk.

13 Zebulun shall dwell by the haven of the sea; he *shall become* a haven for ships, and his border shall adjoin Sidon.

14 "Issachar is a strong donkey, lying down between two burdens.

15 He saw that rest *was* good, and that the land *was* pleasant. He bowed his shoulder to bear *a burden and* became a band of slaves.

16 "Dan shall judge his people as one of the tribes of Israel.

17 Dan shall be a serpent by the way, a viper by the path, that bites the horse's heels so that its rider shall fall backward.

18 I have waited for your salvation, O Lord!

19 "Gad, a troop shall tramp upon him, but he shall triumph at last.

20 "Bread from Asher *shall be* rich, and he shall yield royal dainties.

21 "Naphtali *is* a deer let loose; He uses beautiful words.

22 Joseph *is* a fruitful bough, a fruitful bough by a well; his branches run over the wall.

23 The archers have bitterly grieved him, shot *at him* and hated him.

24 But his bow remained in strength, and the arms of his hands were made strong by the hands of the Mighty *God* of Jacob (From there *is* the Shepherd, the Stone of Israel),

25 By the God of your father who will help you, and by the Almighty who will bless you *with* blessings of heaven above,

Blessings of the deep that lies beneath, blessings of the breasts and of the womb.

26 The blessings of your father have excelled the blessings of my ancestors, up to the utmost bound of the everlasting hills. They shall be on the head of Joseph, and on the crown of the head of him who was separate from his brothers.

27 "Benjamin is a ravenous wolf; in the morning he shall devour the prey, and at night he shall divide the spoil."

28 All these *are* the twelve tribes of Israel, and this *is* what their father spoke to them. and he blessed them; he blessed each one according to his own blessing.

Each son was given their blessing appropriate to him. Some actually received blessings and others received warning of things to come because of their previous actions. After giving his son instructions on where he wanted to be buried, Jacob died peacefully. Joseph's heart was broken after the death of his father. Joseph mourned for his father for forty days and the Egyptians mourned for him for seventy days. After the time of mourning passed, Joseph asked Pharaoh if he could take his father back to Canaan to bury his father, all the dignitaries of his court and all the dignitaries of Egypt accompanied Joseph, his brothers and all that belonged to his father's household except for the children and flock.

Joseph had found great favor in Pharaoh's sight and Pharaoh had great respect for Joseph. After returning to Canaan, Joseph, and those with him built an alter and observed a seven-day mourning period for Jacob. After burying their father, Joseph and all those who traveled to Canaan with him returned to Egypt. The reality of their father being dead begun to settle in and Joseph's brothers feared that Joseph would now try to get revenge on them.

Joseph was not a man of vengeance. He understood his assignment, not only did he understand his assignment, but he willingly accepted his assignment.

Joseph's brothers were so consumed with grief that they couldn't probably believe that all they had did to Joseph that he would not try to get them back. They were so worried about what Joseph would do to them that they sent messengers to Joseph to tell him of their father's wishes.

Genesis 50:16-18

16 So they sent word to Joseph saying, "your father left these instructions before he died

17 This is what you are to say to Joseph; I ask you to forgive your brothers the sins and the wrongs they committed in treating you so badly. Now please forgive the sins of the servants of the God of your father. When their message came to him, Joseph wept.

18 His brothers then came and threw themselves down before him. "We are your slaves," they said.

Hurting his brothers was the farthest thing from Joseph's mind. He assured his brothers that he was not angry with them and that they did not have to be afraid of him. Joseph understood everything had to happen the way it did. He farther assured his brothers that everything evil they did to him God turned it around for his good.

Genesis 50:19-21

19 But Joseph said to them, "don't be afraid. Am I in the place of God?

20 You intended to harm me, but God intended it for good to accomplish what is now being done, the saving of many lives.

21 So then, don't be afraid. I will provide for you and your children." And he reassured them and spoke kindly to them.

Joseph was chosen by God to be hated by his brothers, to be sold into slavery, to be betrayed by his master's wife, thrown into prison, to interpret the dreams of the two most important people of the king of Egypt and later to be placed as second in command of all of Egypt during a time of famine.

Who besides Joseph could have gone through all that he went through and still walk in integrity, humility, character, love, faithfulness, and most of all forgiveness? Joseph had many opportunities to get revenge on his brothers, but he chose not to. Joseph's life had now come full circle.

Final nugget

The roads that we travel on this journey called life will lead us in many different directions. Some roads will take us up the hill and down the hill. Some will be filled with curves, as soon as you're out of one curve you're immediately in another curve. Some roads will be filled with bumps and potholes that will throw you all over the place or shake you up. Some roads will cause you to have to detour and go in a different direction. Some roads may be filled with 4-way stop signs that will cause you to really pay attention, so you will know when it's your turn to go or wait. Some roads may have traffic lights that clearly let you know when to go, stop or precede with caution. Very few roads are smooth and straight forward and all that's required of you is to set the cruise control. No matter which road you find yourself on, know that you are not alone. God is right there willing and waiting to help navigate us through whatever road we find ourselves on. He even provides a few little nuggets along the way to help us learn the best way to travel each road on this journey called life.

www.ingramcontent.com/pod-product-compliance
Lightning Source LLC
Chambersburg PA
CBHW052112110526
44592CB00013B/1579